value to those who love someone who has been diagnosed with mental illness and those who serve the mentally-ill population. Beyond that, it is an enlightening and engaging read for those who those who love real stories about real people. ~ Kathleen Pooler, Reviewer and Author of *Ever Faithful to His Lead: My Journey Away from Emotional Abuse*

NOTHING LIKE NORMAL

SURVIVING A SIBLING'S SCHIZOPHRENIA

Martha Graham-Waldon

A Black Opal Books Publication

GENRE: SELF-HELP/MEMOIRS

NOTHING LIKE NORMAL: Surviving a Sibling's Schizophrenia

Cover Design by Lakshmi Narayan

Print ISBN: 978-1-626943-66-7

First Publication: NOVEMBER 2015

Published by Black Opal Books **http://www.blackopalbooks.com**

DEDICATION

For the Sisters and Brothers

PROLOGUE

When your sibling becomes mentally ill, you feel powerless. The adults are making the decisions—there is not much you can do. It's like being a passenger on a train pummeling toward a certain wreck, witnessing your family plunge into disaster and not being able to step off or change course…

ᏣᏣ

As I stepped over the threshold, the heavy metal door to the psych unit shut with a resounding slam that made me jump. My eyes swept over the drafty expanse of the ward as I searched for her. The faded checkered floor was lit by afternoon shadows. Light spilled into the room like shards of crystal, piercing through the tight wires imbedded in the thick, shatterproof glass.

As I looked at my sister Kathy walking down the corridor toward me, my mind darted back to all that had happened to us both. My once fit, athletic sister was now obese. Her dark hair, usually uncombed and dirty, hung stringy down around her face. Her teeth and nails were stained brown with nicotine.

Suddenly I was caught up short in astonishment. Who was this metamorphosed girl in front of me? Why was she here? Why not me?

I reflected on the past and all that had brought us here…

PART ONE

The Magic

Graham Family, 1959

CHAPTER 1

Kathy Cat and Martha Mouse

Kathy Cat and Martha Mouse lived together in a great big house.

It was always the two of us. The "little girls" they called us.

As close as we were, we were far apart, too, different in so many ways. She was brave and outgoing. I was quiet and introverted. She had long, dark hair that she almost always wore down, tucked behind her ears and flung behind her shoulders. She wore "hang-ten" T-shirts like a uniform, a different one each day. She was dark and beautiful, like an American Indian. Somehow that tiny bit of our Cherokee ancestry was born out in her. In junior high once, a boy signed her yearbook, "To the best Indian girl I know," and we wondered about that.

She was all right till the bump of adolescence sent her careening over the edge. I lost her to a cruel illness that invaded slowly, taking over her bright mind.

This is not only her story. It is the story of a family that was close and then came apart. It is also my story. The story of someone who was in second place, following behind her until I found my own way.

The vortex of my past has sucked me in. Memories flow from a wellspring of dreams…

ઌઌ

I followed behind my sister. She was my leader, my mentor, and the one who showed me the way. We raced into the backyard after elementary school with joyous abandon.

Skipping to the swing, I jumped on and glided carelessly up and down while she headed straight to the tetherball, whacking it powerfully with her fists. Her strength and great athletic ability instilled in me an appreciation for fitness that I carried to this day.

We were best friends for a time, allies within the family, playmates, and confidants. On Saturdays, they would drive us to Seal Beach to attend the Peppermint Playhouse, a wonderful place where we studied ballet, art, and drama. Kathy had a flair for acting and reveled in the musicals we learned and performed there. We sang the themes to "Hello, Dolly," "What Simple Folk Do," from *Camelot* and *Man of La Mancha* as we romped gleefully around the house.

"I am I, Don Quixote, the Lord of La Mancha, my destiny calls and I go!"

She could memorize and recite the Bill of Rights, or a scene from *Hamlet*, with equal flamboyance.

"I challenge you to a duel, *to the death* immediately in the throne room!"

We had a magical childhood. Although we lived in the city, our parents fostered in us a love of nature through wilderness adventures from a very young age. Some summers we hiked in the High Sierras, carrying our gear on backpacks and on pack mules in the backcountry near Yosemite. Tuolome Meadows, Silver Dollar Lake...

Those places were etched upon my memory as clearly as the old photos still hanging on the wall.

As the youngest family members, Kathy and I got to ride on the pack mules when we tired of walking, flopped over on their packs under the bright blue sky beneath the silhouette of white tipped mountain peaks.

During our rest stops and at the end of the day, I rubbed my face against the long nose of Chocolate Charlie, the burro who carried me so loyally during the day's travels.

We waded in icy lakes and streams, baked biscuits in stone ovens, and wrapped and cooked fish in the large leaves picked at Skunk Cabbage Meadow.

Chocolate Charlie, Martha, brother Charlie,
and friends in the Sierras.

Backpacking with pack mules:
Martha and Kathy

We were hiking with another family on a hot summer's day and we stopped in a meadow to rest, drink tepid water from our canteens and fortify ourselves with trail mix or gorp, as we mountaineers called it. I wandered off the dirt path and down to the creek below, which beckoned me with its pleasant gurgling, mixed with the call of bathing wild birds. Crouching down beside the high grass and summer flowers, I took the little wooden boat I had fashioned out of driftwood, with large leaves for a sail, from my knapsack. I launched it into the water again and again, watching the current carry it from eddy to eddy.

I soon lost track of time.

Returning to the trailhead, I was startled to find that there was no one there. In the still silence of the meadow and trees, I began walking up the trail with tears running down my face—obediently blowing the whistle strung around my neck that dad had insisted I always wear. After a while, I saw him hurrying down the hill toward me and he led me up the incline to the waiting group where my mother was beside herself with worry.

At the tender age of five, no psychological damage occurred, and I suffered no resulting abandonment issues from this experience. If anything, it reinforced in me a sense of self-reliance and resourcefulness that I have come to rely upon over the years.

Kathy had her own adventure when she encountered a rattlesnake in the path and bravely steered around it. As a Campfire Girl, she would draw from this incident to name herself "The Brave One" and later she would turn to this well of courage to battle an even more ominous internal adversary.

On a later trek, hiking to the bottom of the Grand Canyon, I led the pack down the trail, skipping merrily ahead and drawing from the inexhaustible wellspring of energy of my seven years. We stopped to rest in the shade of hollows of shale carved out of the canyon walls, sipping from our tin canteens and munching on our trail gorp. The golden sun reflected brilliantly off the rocks while we rested and reveled in the magnificent view, at one with nature and united as a family.

Grand Canyon 1968: Kathy on left,
Jack, Helen, Charlie, Martha

CHAPTER 2

Rambling in the Rambler

"My family is going to Mexico for Christmas!" I was in the first grade and it was show and tell time. I stood up in class and proudly announced the exciting upcoming trip. Our Grandmother was to meet us at the end of our long journey down to Guadalajara, in the heart of old-world Mexico, for a Christmas we would never forget. With two boys, two girls, and our parents, our family of six all fit snuggly into the rambler station wagon that became our home on wheels for two whole weeks.

It was a long drive full of adventures, tantrums, and exotic wonders. In a little hotel by the sea in Mazatlan (dubbed "Monster land" by me), we waded along the shore. My sister and brothers ran wildly in the shining sand. I watched my mother looking young and carefree as she waded into the surf and I called out to her in fear somehow that the waves might steal her away from me. Then she snatched me up, and we spun around joyfully in the lapping white foam. I felt safe—caressed in that tender, fleeting spell of closeness between a mother and child.

Guadalajara was a new world for us. We explored the colorful market place, marveling at the wares in each and every stall. This was where we shopped for Christmas and when the day arrived, our presents were wrapped in newspaper around a makeshift tree. Kathy and I received brown-skinned marionettes, a boy with a sombrero and blue-checkered shirt, a girl with brown braids and a white muslin dress. We walked them up and down the stairs of our two-story hotel, making them dance jerkily to strains of music from a nearby bar.

"Stay in the hotel, *chiquitas*!" the owner of the hotel warned us one day, telling us there was a caravan of gypsies down the road who might kidnap us.

We were not really frightened but stuck around the hotel that day just to be on the safe side.

There was a piñata, likely for my brother's birthday two days after Christmas. Some local children joined in the fun as we swung at it repeatedly with a bat. I struck aimlessly and blindly when it was my turn, barely glazing the side of the swinging donkey.

Now it was Kathy's turn. After they tied the blindfold over her face, she powerfully connected with the bat as it tore open the papier-mâché neck of the colorful beast. Candy and paper streamers flew out in all directions as a mad scramble for the sweet loot ensued.

That night in the hotel where we were thriftily sharing rooms, Grandmother and I were in one bed sound asleep when I suddenly sat bolt upright.

"Well, go on, go to the bathroom quickly!"

I made it just in time to vomit up the colorful candy that tasted so delicious just a few hours before.

We visited with family friends in what seemed to me to be a huge tiled palace. We met with a matador and my brother whispered to me that the man had a crush on my mother.

It was at nearby Lake Chapala that Kathy revealed one of her first fears. My brave sister seemed to have a fear of the water and boats.

"No, no, Daddy, let's go back!"

She was panicking as the small boat shifted from side to side when the blue waves lapped up against it. The horizon was far beyond the immense body of water that surrounded us. Mom comforted Kathy until we finally reached the shore again.

On the long drive home, the rambler broke down, prolonging our trip and allowing us to experience even more of Mexico's charms. My mother would later write about this misadventure in a short story entitled "Ring Job at Obregon," which won an award.

At the end of those vacations, we were dirty, tired, and full of memories that would last a lifetime.

ᏋᏋ

While some families tossed out "I love yous" daily like dime store candy, ours were carefully and copiously measured out, frugally saved for special moments. Yet even though the words were seldom spoken, the love between my parents was clear.

I treasured the memories of my parents and the great love they had for each other. Though we were not very demonstrative with our love and certainly not as effusive as some, we were a close-knit and happy family, especially in those early years.

My soft-spoken father gave my mother subtle messages of his devotion to her. He would come in the door after walking home from work—lean and handsome, carrying his suit jacket draped over his shoulder, his face slightly moist with sweat—and plant a kiss upon my mother and then one on my cheek. One day, he presented her with a bouquet of flowers and they kissed, not passionately, but a heartfelt peck.

He would use a Spanish expression (one of only a few he knew), "*Yo te amo*," to let her know he loved her. Once he wrote it in the cylinder of a pen he gave her, like a secret code. It was these understated expressions of love which defined their relationship. They were in sync—

both of them whistling merrily at opposite ends of the house on weekends, until their melodies wove together into a perfect harmony.

Of my mother, I remember the things she liked in those early days—her "Straw Hat" perfume that we would buy her for Mother's Day and her birthday and the packs of Wrigley's spearmint gum she kept stashed in the kitchen drawers along with blue chip stamps to cash in.

She called me "dear heart" when I was good and Mom lovingly invented nicknames for all her children when we were small. She also made up cute little nonsensical songs for each of us.

"Moopery Lou, Mooperly Lou, miperly maperly, I love you."

She called me "moop" even after I had grown up, although I have never known why. Maybe it was because I would mope around a bit…

Kathy's nickname, "Kathryn MacGonigiggle" was fun loving with a matching tune:

"Kathryn Macgonigiggle, piggle, sniggle, wiggle, niggle. Kathryn Macgonigiggle, piggle sniggle, pooh."

My oldest brother's jingle was taken from a folk tune. "Twiddle diddle dumplings, my son John!" while middle brother Charlie's was a true original, "Chuck-a-walla-boomstick!"

☙❧

As my mother strode into the living room dressed up

for the evening and smelling nice, with her heels clicking, it was a clue that she was about to depart for a "meeting" of one sort or another and that we would likely be left with a baby sitter. We never minded, since we knew we would play games until well past bedtime.

CHAPTER 3

Born into Grief

At the tender age of four or five, I learned (probably from my older brothers and sister) about my other sister, Louise, who died shortly before I was born. She had a birth defect in that her brain was not completely formed. Mom kept a picture of her as a baby on her dresser for many years. In that photo, she lay in my mother's arms, gazing up at her with adoring eyes. Physically she looked like a beautiful, normal infant but she didn't have control over her limbs and would never walk. She died at Porterville State Hospital when she was four years old. Thus I was born during a time of great sadness. My birth was unplanned, although having another infant was a comfort for my mother and father in their time of grief.

ᴕᴕ

I was little and still not in school. I drew a man's shoulders and round head with a top hat in black crayon on the green Formica kitchen counter top. I drew checkers on his suit and, carried away with my artistry, continued the squares across his face and top hat as well. Mom was so tickled by this that she didn't clean it up, leaving it to show to dad when he got home.

That was the day I suddenly became overcome with grief at the loss of Louise, a sister I would never know. I didn't know what brought the deluge on but after showing my artwork off, I cried and cried, sobbing to my parents, "Why did she have to die?"

Mom and Dad embraced me, held me, and mom cried too.

"She's got it, Jack…"

"It" was the grief that was still so fresh and real in their lives.

CHAPTER 4

Treasured Memories

Graham Kids: Charlie, Martha, Kathy,
John on an adventure in Arizona.

Through it all, the happy memories somehow outshone the bad.

It was a place where we played in summers that seemed to last forever. I joyfully rode my purple stingray, with streamers on the handlebars, up and down the street, through the alleyways and the nooks and crannies at the white church on the corner. Up and down the overpass at the community college at the end of the street, through the empty open halls at my mission-style elementary school, sometimes pausing to lie in the grass or play in the empty playground.

The memories are shadows that become sharp and clear like photos in a chemical bath—my sister kissing me goodbye on the front porch, as she left for school with all the big kids, while I stayed behind, awaiting her return for our little tea parties on the curb.

And a clear picture of us as little girls when mom would cut our hair into pixie, bowl type cuts as we fidgeted on the patio in the noonday sun.

I was right behind her as we scaled the tall, sappy tree at the side of the house. Within the boughs of that tree, we reached a dark and secret spot where Kathy had stashed a pack of cigarettes in an old drawstring purse.

"Come on, Marth. Smoke with me," she entreated me as she held out a long white Pall Mall.

As I gingerly placed the cylinder between my lips, Kathy lit it skillfully with a match, just like our elegant aunt would, the ember growing red as I timidly inhaled. Then I was overcome with a cough racking through my small body. I had never felt so horrible!

The horrible and nauseous sensation that swept over me cured me forever from this vice (until I discovered marijuana at the age of fourteen). Yet that early encounter with nicotine may have drawn in Kathy, who later became addicted in the state hospital.

We would "surf" on the dark blue carpeting of our bedroom, using the long bolster pillows from our twin beds as surfboards. I know this must have been Kathy's idea. She was always the active, athletic one, balancing on the imaginary waves with her long black hair swept back, her arms spread out in the perfect surfer pose.

We were a handful. We bounced endlessly on our beds until Mom or Dad forced us to settle down and crawl into them when they came to tuck us in.

We giggled ourselves to sleep or went on a midnight adventure.

"Martha, are you asleep? Want to go to the bar?"

"Sure."

Then we rose, stealthily creeping to the bathroom next door where we'd fill a soapy glass from the sink and send the "beer" sliding along the side of porcelain tub "bar" to the one waiting, seated on the toilet barstool next to the clothes hamper bar.

CHAPTER 5

Insomnia

Kathy and I lay in our twin beds in the velvety darkness of our little room, waiting for sleep and the respite of dreams.

"Are you asleep, Martha?" she called to me and I sensed the desperation in her tone.

I was actually lost in my imagination. Until I was about seven or so, I could easily review the memories of my short life and I often played them in my mind like a movie.

Her voice broke through my reverie.

"Not yet," I said. "What's wrong?"

"I *can't* sleep. It *won't* come."

"Think of something nice; think about your favorite teacher at school or something."

A long silence followed. I pulled my blankets close around me as the vivid images and happy memories returned to play out beneath my closed eyelids.

"*Mommm!*" Kathy called out loudly, her voice echoing down the hallway and into the far corners of our home.

Mom came quickly as she always did when Kathy's hysteria surfaced, always unannounced and demanding our full attention. She sat down beside Kathy on the bed. "What's the matter?"

"I *can't* sleep, Mom. I've been trying for over an hour."

Mom lay down beside her and began to speak reassuringly. "Just close your eyes and clear your mind, don't think about sleeping, just relax."

The three of us lay there together for what seemed like another hour, only now Kathy began to whimper and protest some more. Mom went next door to the bathroom and came back with some aspirin and a glass of water. "This will help," she said as she gave the pill to her despairing daughter.

"How will that help, Mom?"

"It makes your aches and pains go away and then your body will relax and sleep."

This must have been convincing and true because, after what seemed like forever, we suddenly awoke to the cheerful light of morning bursting through the window as our parakeets sang out and welcomed in the new day.

ଓଡଓଡ

To escape on our own, to experience true freedom and not want to come home—it was our imaginations that propelled us as we played kick the can, hide and seek, and performed original plays beneath a curtain of green tendrils hanging from the weeping willow tree in our front yard.

On Saturday mornings before it got light, our neighbor Sandy came to knock on our bedroom window for our "nature walks" in the middle of the suburbs. My eyes were glued shut with sleep as I slowly recognized her. Then Kathy and I would rise, pull on some clothes, and the climb out the bedroom window.

The three of us would stealthily creep into our back yard. From there we ascended onto the red stucco walls surrounding our home and slowly crept along, observing everything.

We passed by each neighbor's yard, surveying whatever we could. We saw cats slinking around in the sunrise, beautiful rose gardens in the sparkling dew, and the breaking light of dawn lent an air of mystery to it all.

For me, this dovetailed with my obsession with the novel *Harriet the Spy* by Louise Fitzhugh. I was Harriet, carrying my notebook and spying as I scribbled down the suspicious comings and goings of our neighbors in the intrigue of suburbia.

ଔଔ

A gaggle of eleven-year-old girls convened in the middle of the block and marched up to the community college pool where we waited in line, impatiently shifting from foot to foot as we chatted incessantly. The pool opened. We paid our dollar and were each given a locker key to wear around our necks on wet dangling strings.

We swam amid a throng of swarming young bodies under the watchful eye of the lifeguard. I was the smallest and she signaled me out with a loud toot of her whistle.

"You! Show me that you can swim."

I awkwardly kicked my feet and forced my arms into a classic free stroke, even though dog paddling was my usual modus operandi.

She waved me off. "Okay."

As we left the pool, my lungs ached with each intake of breath. I found this effect of over chlorination interesting, instead of concerning, and headed happily home, glad for the fun and friends, feeling that I had proved myself worthy.

CHAPTER 6

Last Born

Within our family, I struggled to prove myself too. Being the youngest child was a unique condition—as the last-born I was coddled and fussed over, and the older siblings tried to look after me. Still, I was at the bottom of the teasing chain with no one below me that I could pass along the torment to. In my defense, I learned how to use the cuteness factor to my advantage. If there were treats, they would give me the last one as well as special gifts from family friends. A tiny thing, I could lay claim to the prime spot on Mom's lap when we gathered around the TV in the family room.

As we grew older, I tagged along behind my brothers and sister, struggling to be a part of the fun. But more often than not, I would end up alone left to my own devices and free to create my own world. In my world as a six year old, our house was full of fun diversions.

After dinner, I grabbed a knife, fork, and spoon from the kitchen and snuggled up in a small round chair in the living room next to the bay window. Hours went by as I played with my imaginary family. The knife was the defender, the daddy, the rounded spoon the perfect mom, and the fork, a teen-aged daughter with spiky long hair. If I tired of my flatware family, there were always the real dolls beckoning from the doll cabinet that Grandmother had brought us from her travels to transport me to all corners of the globe. Or I could grab my skipper doll with the long brown legs and play with her on my pillow at night.

In the bed next to mine, Kathy was laying out her beloved "Damn It" dolls. They were troll-like beings with felt clothes that she collected. Otherwise, she didn't have much use for all the dolls. After school, she could make "creepy crawlers," which were plastic bugs and creatures that she would "bake" in a mold while I sat and played, enamored with my Easy Bake Oven.

The dolls and toys would keep me amused until I discovered the joys of reading in grade school and books became my best friends. I would read one I brought home from the school library each night, curled up and happy, an island unto myself.

On Saturday mornings, I rose before the others, grabbing a blanket and curling up in front of the TV to watch cartoons, an activity that my siblings seemed to have outgrown. Sometimes I would head to the Saturday matinee alone or with friends from the neighborhood, first buying candy and comic books to haul along. I was going for the life of the All-American kid, carefree and happy-go-lucky, trying my best to ignore any of the troubles surrounding me.

ᏋᏋ

"Do those girls have beetles in their hair?"

I was looking at the black and white photo on the front page of the local paper spread across the coffee table. It showed young girls with long hair whipping around their faces. They appeared to be screaming and writhing in pain.

"No, dear. That's all about a new band called the Beatles from England."

The British "Invasion" soon arrived onto our family hi-fi, and I watched as my sister and her friends danced around the house, mesmerized by the catchy, hypnotic tunes.

"She loves you, yeah, yeah, yeah!"

Soon I was joining in and as always, I wanted to do whatever the older kids did.

We soon began accumulating fan club paraphernalia, like pins and bobble heads of my favorite, Paul, and of Ringo, who Kathy had a thing for. But while we loved to listen to records, it was even more fun to sing to ourselves.

"Hello, Dolly! Well, hello, Dolly! It's so nice to have you back where you belong!"

Besides Beatlemania, we loved performing Broadway musicals, learning all the lyrics at the Peppermint Playhouse on Saturdays or on the special occasions when our parents treated the family to a musical like *Man of La Mancha* and later to more hip shows like *Simon and Garfunkel*, a family favorite, at the Long Beach arena.

CHAPTER 7

Watching the Boob Tube

On occasional lazy Saturdays, we watched TV or as Dad called it, "The Boob Tube", in the darkened family room, lounging on the down-filled couch that once belonged to movie star Burt Lancaster, a gift passed down to us by the minister of our church's family. I loved to burrow down deep into the hollows of downy pillows until no one could see me, like a rabbit in my own personal hole. We would rise from our reverie occasionally, to raid the kitchen for snacks such as cinnamon toast. Like a mother lion surrounded by her cubs, mother and children rested contentedly in the cave we called home.

On weekday afternoons after homework, we watched our favorites TV shows. *Lost in Space* and *Batman,* bleeding into the evening news for Dad, followed by *The Flintstones*, which was eventually replaced by the sci-fi epoch *Star Trek* or the very "in" *Laugh-in*. When the reception went fuzzy, my oldest brother or Dad whacked the top of the old black and white, being careful not to knock off the rabbit ears. This usually restored the picture to an acceptable level of clarity. But that old TV brought more than entertainment into our home as we witnessed history unfold on its round, brown screen.

ശ്ര

In November 1963, we were transfixed to the TV like the rest of America as we first learned of the assassination of President Kennedy and later watched his funeral procession.

I watched my mother break down in tears as little John-John brought his baby-like hand to his brow in a military salute to his father. Later, the shooting of Bobby Kennedy, shown so starkly on the screen, caused Mom to sob silently in horror. A little older by then, I placed my hand upon her shoulder in a comforting, grown-up way. A civil rights activist, Mom was also devastated by the murder of Martin Luther King Jr.

On that day, too upset to cook, she went to pick up some hamburgers for us at McDonalds. She stepped up to the counter after waiting in line for a while.

"So, did ya hear they finally got him?" The teenager

behind the counter was nonchalant, speaking over his shoulder to a coworker behind him.

This was too much for Mom. She began to cry and immediately turned around and went to the back of the line, trying to compose herself. Then she had to face him again to place her order.

“I’m sorry, lady.” Now the kid seemed sheepish, like a little boy who had just become aware of the harsh world waiting beyond the golden arches.

CHAPTER 8

More About Mom

My mom, Helen, was in charge, in control, firmly steering the helm of our family. She relished this power and reveled in all the fruits of her labor as she proudly watched her brood of sons and daughters grow. Having earned an MBA in sociology from Columbia, she had an academic leaning and struggled to find an outlet for it in her writing, teaching, and community activism.

She did all those things well, organizing after-school Spanish classes for the neighborhood kids while working as a substitute teacher.

We would cringe when they called her in to substitute for one of our classes. For me, that only happened once and I ended up feeling proud when I saw how she skillfully took control of my junior high English class.

She and I were especially close during my childhood. She made sure that Kathy and I had the requisite ballet and tap lessons, as well as the opportunity of leading our Campfire Girl groups, and she made sure to send us to winter and summer camps. She created family traditions, like making grape jelly from the Concord grapes growing on the vines in the backyard and hosting Ukrainian Easter Egg parties with our adopted Ukrainian grandmother, actually a dear family friend.

Mom had high standards for us and for everyone she met. She abhorred hearing profanities and created her own arsenal of substitute swear words. Some of her favorites were "Oh, pickle," "son of a peanut," "fersling-ing," and when she was really mad, an emphatically placed "Oh, *plut*."

This anti-curse campaign became her personal vendetta but, despite her efforts, she was not able to purge us of vulgarities and create a swear-free zone. Once she scolded a neighborhood boy with a ten-minute lecture for "polluting her air" with his foul language.

Like many women of her era, she was unfulfilled on some level in her role as wife and mother. She wanted to publish a book, based on her research on the human behaviors of blame and reprisal, but the demands of family kept her from achieving this goal.

Once or twice, she was able to escape from the constraints of suburban life when Grandmother would whisk her off on a cruise. A housekeeper was hired to take care of us during these adventures and these welcome breaks helped her maintain her sanity, providing her respite from the never-ending demands of a large family.

Entering middle age in the turbulent Vietnam War era, Mom felt torn by a desire to conform to the laws of the land or be swept up in the protests of the day as she faced the possibility of her sons being drafted.

Like most mothers, she was saddled with the impossible task of trying to be everything to everybody. The struggle between her own ambitions and family demands, along with some menopausal hormones tossed into the mix, caused her to lash out unexpectedly, at times turning on a dime and puzzling us all.

One night, I returned home a little late from a party with my junior high friends, almost proud of my slowly budding social life.

"Why didn't you *call*? You don't know what it's like to worry about someone!" She had grabbed me by the shoulders and was shaking me, her horrified face inches away from mine.

"But I'm only thirty minutes late!" I pulled away from her, not expecting such dire consequences, and then retreated to the bedroom that Kathy and I shared, commiserating with her about why Mom had to give us such a hard time.

ɞɞ

Mom wanted to know why we couldn't be like the girls in so and so's family, as if this was our fault. The criticisms increased as we got older. She was particularly disapproving of the way we dressed, adding to the insecurity I was already feeling in attempting to blend in at junior high. Under her reproachful glances, I felt like I could not please her no matter how hard I tried.

After a long day she sat at the dining room table in the evenings, sipping wine and writing in pencil on plain white tablets—line after line, scrolling down until the pages were full, bursting with words, filled with her observations on the world and sometimes rife with anger and criticisms of people and local politics.

Her gift of writing and her passion for it was passed down like a torch to us kids.

CHAPTER 9

Portrait of Dad

Monday July 5, 1965

Dear Kathy,

I hope that you have had a good holiday on the fourth of July. Did you? What do you do at camp to celebrate this kind of holiday? I imagine that they do not allow fireworks in the forest. Did you have a big campfire at night?

We set off some wonderful fireworks in the back yard. Small pin wheels, Big pinwheels, Whistling Petes, Fountains of Light, Glowing Snakes, Colored Sparklers...These were some of the things we set off in our backyard. Also, we could look down the street and watch the beautiful sky rockets, at the stadium, at the college. The last one we set off was a tremendous fountain of light, which sent bright showers of light as high as the house in red, white, and blue colors. (The dogs were frightened and hid themselves).

We were sad because you weren't here with us (even though we're glad that you are able to be at Camp Wintonka). We saved a box of sparklers and some glowing snakes for you.

Love,

Daddy

Dad was the one who made it all possible. He designed the unforgettable vacations and the weekend excursions to amazing places. He led us on backpacking trips into the wilderness and was a well-respected leader of the Sierra Club.

Dad was the provider and, from his efforts, we wanted for nothing. We had plenty of food on the table, music lessons, and sports uniforms—everything we asked for we duly received. With four kids, it could not have been easy but he worked hard every day, trudging to and from the office without a complaint.

When summer came and the rest of the family got to lollygag around the house, he enjoyed our leisure vicariously, reveling in the more relaxed atmosphere of our home, trading his workplace necktie for peace beads on the weekends, when he was relaxed and happy.

A gentle and kind man who loved nature, his voice and presence had always been reassuring, when I would confide in him about my inner turmoil. He held a special tenderness for his little girls—Kathy was his kitten and I was his mouse.

Dad's interest in classical guitar became a family tradition and my brothers learned to play intricate duets with him and each other in beautiful harmonies. He was strong yet frequently silent—allowing my mother to take over with her words and control the family reins, as she was apt to do.

CHAPTER 10

Shards of Tragedy

While we look at childhood as a shrine of innocence, it is always fractured by the cracks of life's pain and loss that allow the shards of tragedy to slip through. ~ MGW

೧೧

On long weekends and at Easter, our family drove to Bakersfield to be with our cousins, the whole clan together, with the kids' ages staggered so closely together that it was like a jumble of brothers and sisters to play with carelessly in the hills and backyards of our kin.

Thanksgivings were usually at our house, with the families surrounding our huge pine table. My grandfather—who we called "Grandpa Pete," although that was not his name—sat near the head of table smoking his pipe, his eyes twinkling with happiness at the sight of all his offspring together. He had lead a rough and tumble life, never getting over the break up with my father's mother. He had insisted on raising his four kids alone, going so far as to hide them from his ex-wife through frequent moves around Texas. Along the way, he had developed a quirky sense of humor and loved to tease us by calling us bizarre names like "Prunella" and "Oswald."

When my Uncle Don died, taken by a sudden heart attack at a young and vibrant age, Grandpa Pete was joking at the funeral as usual. "Automatic door openers" was his comment when the man in the black suit held the door open to our funeral car.

From my little corner in the backseat of the limo, I thought back to my memory of my handsome uncle with his jet-black hair holding Kathy, my cousin Kim, and me, all up on his strong wide shoulders. Then we were led into the funeral parlor where we sat solemnly, as tissues were passed around and a eulogy said. This was my first funeral.

A shiver ran up and down my spine as I stood up on my tiptoes and peered in at my uncle's body lying prone upon white satin as we filed past his coffin during the viewing.

At the gravesite, I looked up as he was lowered into the ground and saw my cousin Kim smiling at me lovingly. I watched my Aunt Betty, his widow, holding her younger sister who was wracked with sobs.

I learned more about death when our next-door neighbor took his own life by leaving their sedan running in the garage. It happened when I was very young (probably around six). That house was between the neighbors and us, where I would play. I was there with my friends in their backyard, playing with Barbies and GI Joes—happy couples driving toy jeeps in the dirt under their huge backyard tree—when their mother came grimly out of the house and headed toward us. "Martha, you may as well hear this too."

Then she told us of his death.

We could hear his wife, Sadie wailing in grief next door.

The next day, her grandson, a little boy named Mikey arrived from Arizona and, as we swung on rope swings slowly and rhythmically, he sighed. "My grandmother has been crying and crying all day."

I later learned this little boy had leukemia and he must have died as well. I remember the translucence of his skin and I could see the blue veins below the surface.

There was so much tragedy there on Whitehurst Ave and so many memories there still.

CHAPTER 11

Grandmother

Our family was solid but full of contradictions—a rock of traditionalism and liberalism melded together. Our parents were from Texas and my mother's mother, a fine southern lady who came to visit us for at least one month each year, had a large influence on our rearing. "Grandmother" was what we called her, never Grandma, no, that casual title would be unbefitting to a lady of her stature.

Grandmother's generosity extended well beyond her lifetime in the memories and gifts she bestowed on her offspring. She worked for Scholastic Publishing and, every summer, large cartons of paperbacks would arrive for us to peruse through and read—something I thoroughly enjoyed.

Grandmother always came from Texas to see us at Christmas and driving to the airport in Los Angeles to pick her up was a big occasion. As we drove past the oil rigs and industrial plants along the freeway, that were ugly polluters during the day, she was enchanted by the image of them lit up and twinkling as we drove home in the night.

"Like fairy palaces," Grandmother said, as I tried to the picture the imaginary fairies and elves that might live there.

Since it was the holiday season, she would be wearing her special silver bell earrings. We loved to see and hear them ring as she shook her head from side to side, to our delight.

Her snowy white, perfectly coiffed hair hardly moved as she walked around our house. She always wore dresses that fell below the knee with solid, low-heeled shoes to boost her petite stature.

One afternoon during her visit, I heard her heels clicking on the hardwood floor as we prepared to go to a holiday service at our church. Grandmother appeared wearing a fox stole around her shoulders, its face intact with a clasp in its mouth that fastened onto its own tail.

"Can I pet it?"

She nodded and I ran my fingers over its silky fur with morbid fascination.

Grandmother was careful to cultivate special relationships with all her grandchildren and, as the youngest,

I got to spend a lot of time with her. One year she took me to the mall, which was about a half mile from our home. We walked to Bullocks, one of the anchor department stores of the time, to see a fashion show and have lunch.

Although I don't recall much of the fashion show, I do remember the lunch we ordered. One item on the menu intrigued me.

"It says a peach moose," I pointed out to Grandmother. "How can that be?"

"It's a dessert," she explained. "Do you want one?"

So she ordered it for me and, to this day, I can remember the marvelous creamy texture and sweet, peachy flavor. A wonderful thing, indeed.

As we headed home from the mall, Grandmother asked me not to tell my mom how far we had walked, since she would be concerned about her weak heart.

"Yes, Grandmother."

I thanked her for the special treat and day we had shared.

ꟹ

Grandmother loved to travel and she had been around the world three times. She always said she had "itchy feet" and needed to take at least one trip a year. As the youngest of four, I learned that I would be given a trip to Europe in my teens.

I witnessed first my brothers, and then Kathy, take

the trips that were Grandmother's gifts to each one of us.

After each of her own frequent trips, she would bring back a doll from every country for us girls that would go in a special cabinet. I loved to play with these until I reached an age where playing with dolls no longer seemed cool.

On the large globe in our living room, she showed me the many continents and countries she had traveled to. I would return to it often, spinning it randomly and running my fingers over the bumpy surfaces of the mountains and the smooth surfaces of the blue oceans. Mysterious, incredible countries were an endless source of fascination for me.

"Tell me about Greenland," I asked her. This huge island sitting far up at the top of the world was one of my favorite countries to ponder. "Is it all green?"

It turned out Grandmother had never been there but we looked it up in the encyclopedia and I later wrote a report about it for elementary school.

Many summers the family would drive to Texas to visit Grandmother in San Antonio. The long, hot trip in our rambler station wagon was full of adventures along the way. We passed through desolate mountain and desert towns and stopped to explore any interesting tourist traps and national monuments en route.

"Almost there."

We read the Stuckey's billboards along the road that created an impending sense of expectation for us hot and sticky travelers. "You are here!" the final sign announced and we clamored out of the car and into the restaurant like a hungry herd of cattle.

Carlsbad Caverns in New Mexico was one stop over where we were able to cool off as we wandered, dazed, among the amazing stalactites and stalagmites adorning the cave walls. This was one of many wonders on the route, including the colossal Hoover Dam.

As we arrived in San Antonio and pulled into Grandmother's driveway in the predawn hours, having slept in the rambler while Mom and Dad drove through the night, I pressed my face against the window and started to open the door.

"Shhh!"

They warned us to lie still and be quiet until sunrise. Looking out the window, we watched a cat stealthily tracking and then pouncing on a mouse in the narrow driveway, toying with the little brown prey in its paws.

Suddenly the porch light turned on and out came Grandmother with outstretched arms, welcoming us into the three-story home where she raised my mother. Kathy and I tumbled into the large four-poster bed that had been Mom's while the boys got to stay in the upstairs attic apartment. That night, we girls giggled and jumped on the huge bed long into the night.

The house was large and elegant, filled with beautiful historic antiques. There was a parlor to chat in as we sat perched on embroidered high-back chairs and a Victorian sofa. Adjoining this was a formal dining room with a huge long table, sideboards, and a swinging door that led into the kitchen.

The entry door opened from the front porch and into a wide hallway with the parlor on the right and an office and library on the left. A sloping banister led up the main stairs at the end of the hall to the two upper levels, but there was also a smaller set of wooden stairs, as if designed for servants, which descended back down into the kitchen.

The next morning I crept down the wooden stairs and paused at the bottom, hiding behind the wooden clapboard divider and peered over, "spying," as Grandmother prepared our breakfast.

"I see you there, Martha. Come on down."

A teacher for many years, Grandmother must have developed "eyes in the back of her head."

The kitchen looked unchanged since the Depression, with an old icebox, a pantry, and large black and white checkered tiles gracing the floor. We ate in the dining room, which stayed cool in the summer heat behind heavy drapes. We sat in antique chairs beneath the constant hum from the whirring blades of the ceiling fan overhead.

Right next door was a fire station with a huge bell that the firemen would let us ring after we tired of clamoring onto the sideboards of their red fire engine.

We drank from Coke bottles that we brought upstairs, visited the Alamo and relatives, and had the time of our lives during those long hot summers.

ᏅᏅ

"Mom, there's something behind my ear."

I ran my finger over what felt like a smooth lump but turned out to be a small colony of ticks. Grandmother knew the remedy for this and firmly held a match up to my ear until they dislodged themselves one by one.

Always accident prone, I also got bit on my cheek by a dog on the sidewalk in front of the house. I once woke up screaming in the middle of the night when I discovered a blister on my chest from the heat. My brothers came running down the landing from the attic, as all the kids stood assembled in the hall to see what the excitement was about.

Grandmother's younger brother, who we called Uncle Billy, had a vacation home at Lake Medina outside of San Antonio. Staying there was like a little paradise for us kids.

The house was set back from the lake with a long, sloping lawn of crab grass leading down to a dock at the water's edge. Upon our arrival, we kids climbed into our bathing suits and raced down the lawn, onto the dock, and jumped, splashing into the lake with wild abandon.

Across the water were walls of cliffs that we explored further in a motorboat, with my older brothers at the helm, their long hair hanging down below their ears, their shoulders tanned by the summer sun. The clear humid air was cut by the oily smell of gasoline from the outboard motor. We watched the swallows dart in and out of the hollows in the rock where they nested. We went water skiing endlessly around the lake, finally letting loose of the reins and floating into the shore as if walking on water.

Most amazing of all were the evenings when, after enjoying a meal together, we sat in the living room and watched the animals. Uncle Billy threw kernels of corn from a bucket all over the lawn at dusk and then banged loudly on the bucket, letting all the creatures know it was time to come and get it. We sat, looking out through the floor-to-ceiling windows, mesmerized as deer, raccoons, quail, and armadillos came to feed. I don't remember there being a TV there but I know for sure we didn't miss it.

Uncle Billy's Lake. Martha and Kathy

CHAPTER 12

Endless Summer

It was the summer of 1968, close enough to the summer of love that its strains floated through the air to the back of our Dodge van, where Kathy and I lay prone on the platform bed my parents had installed for this cross country "heritage" trip.

"Come on people now, smile on your brother. Everybody get together, try and love one another right now, right now, right nowww…"

There was pop music from the Archies. "Sugar, ah, honey-honey. You are my candy girl and you got me wanting you."

Dad had carefully planned our itinerary to see all the historic places we had only read about—Boston, Plymouth Rock, Jamestown, Niagara Falls, even New York

City. The days were long in the back of the van but our arrival at each KOA campground or destination filled us with thrills and sudden energy as we romped through museums or cannonballed into swimming pools.

In the southwest portion of the trip we stayed at a dude ranch in Wyoming. Riding along the trail on horseback, our guide led the way as jack rabbits scurried from the chaparral and out of our path. One afternoon, we threw our fishing lines into a stocked pond. Within moments, Kathy pulled out a flopping and twisting trout and then swung her line directly behind her, which cast her shimmering catch directly into my face!

"*Kathy*!" I protested in irritation but, eventually, we collapsed wildly with laughter, having the time of our lives.

My oldest brother, in a sullen teenage phase, had insisted on staying home on this trip while my brother Charlie rode shotgun next to dad, helping to navigate with huge unfurled road maps. Perhaps as a reward, Charlie got to buy a sticker for each state we entered, which he affixed to the rear side window—Arizona, Nevada, Wyoming, Utah, Texas, Virginia, Massachusetts. Soon the colorful stickers filled the window. At the end of that marvelous month, we would have visited 36 states *and* Canada. When school started, I would brag about this to all my friends.

Somewhere in the middle of the country, Kathy snapped after a fight someone had. She opened the door to the van, stepped out, and started walking away down a deserted road. "That hippie was right, man, I just need to do my own thing," she called back to us, remembering a vagabond we met somewhere along the way.

Somehow, I was used to these outbursts from my sister and was not alarmed. Or I hid my fear, just like I hid under the furniture when my father and brother raised their voices in their occasional shouting matches of anger.

Eventually, Kathy climbed back into the van and we continued on our journey.

This was the summer when I was haunted by a perplexing question, which I couldn't shake from my mind.

Who made God?

Kathy and I had metaphysical talks on this subject as we rolled through fields and plains.

One day after we tire of playing road bingo, we pass each other notes in the back of the van.

Do you ever think about who made the sky? her note to me reads.

I recalled a story I wrote in third grade about the Easter Bunny spilling his blue paint bucket across the sky while making Easter eggs and quickly scribbled an abbreviated version down that I passed back to her.

"People have wondered about these things for centuries. You are wise to think of that."

Her appreciative response made me feel good about myself. I smiled and then settled in for a nap.

Yet my nagging thoughts about creationism prevailed throughout our travels and they would lead me on a continuing spiritual journey as I grew up.

CHAPTER 13

The Monkey and the Menagerie

Along with two growing boys and two growing girls came an ever-multiplying parade of pets. First off, there was Snowball, who, in spite of her name, was a black and white spotted Cocker Spaniel mix. She joined the family as a puppy long before I was even conceived.

Cats were not allowed, due to my grandmother's serious allergy, even though she visited only about once a year, but this was made up for by a proliferation of all manner of other beasts.

The rodent contingent included hamsters, a pair of rats, and a little white mouse in honor of my nickname, "Martha Mouse." Two parakeets resided in a large white cage in the bedroom that Kathy and I shared. When we opened their cage door, the colorful birds fluttered happily around our little room, returning to the safety of their cage when they grew weary and hungry. One day, a sad collision with the bedroom door and a broken neck ended Kathy's bird, Chipper's, life.

We buried him in the backyard along with the other deceased creatures but, later, bought her a new bird to keep mine company.

Our desert tortoise had that whole yard to traverse slowly until he disappeared one day, never to be seen again. His fate remains a mystery.

Bomba came into our lives when my oldest brother John discovered her at the local pet shop. She was a Wooly Monkey imported from South America by a merchant marine who had kept her in his garage until he could no longer care for her.

My brother, appealing to my mom's love of animals, got permission to buy her, complete with a cage and little monkey clothes, for a very reasonable price. And so it was that we came to be the only family on the block, or possibly in the town, to have a pet monkey!

As the youngest, I loved Bomba like a little sibling I never had. She was so tame at first, actually sitting at the kitchen table with Mom and me for lunch when the older kids lingered at school.

She could wear a little diaper and pajamas and would even use the toilet if placed on it at the exact right moment. She would cuddle up in our arms, holding her beloved pineapple-shaped mug close to her body on the Burt Lancaster down-filled couch.

As she grew larger, we had a big outdoor cage built, as long and large as one you might see in a zoo. We connected it to the smaller indoor cage through a window so Bomba got the best of both worlds—joining us inside in the family room—or swinging outside from her ropes and swings, depending upon her mood.

In an old black and white photo, I kneel crouched in the corner of the outdoor cage, as timid as my nickname of mouse, while Kathy plays boldly with Bomba, her arms outstretched toward the monkey until it jumps downs to her and she swings her around enthusiastically in the air.

Bomba, who looked an awful lot like Curious George, seemed to grow more mischievous with time. She learned to open the clip lock on her indoor cage and wreaked havoc on the house one day when no one was home, unfurling the toilet paper in the bathroom and even tearing some of the wallpaper off the wall.

Luckily for her, we were not fastidious housekeepers and, although we scolded her, this incident was taken in stride and we simply looked for a better lock for her cage.

Still, she persevered and would somehow get out, crawl through Snowball's doggy door, climb up the fig tree, and swing onto our roof. From there it was easy for her to traverse the trees and gleefully romp on all the surrounding rooftops.

"The monkey's loose! The monkey's loose!"

All the children in the neighborhood gathered together, pointing at Bomba, who was standing up straight on her hind legs, looking down at us calmly, as if to say tauntingly, "Catch me if you can!"

Well, most of the time, we couldn't and waited until Bomba finally tired of these antics and walked civilly up to the front door, stretching her long, prehensile tail up like a leash to be led back into the house.

Once a neighbor spotted her through his kitchen window, causing the poor old man to nearly suffer heart failure in surprise.

All we could do was apologize and try to clean up whatever messes she might leave behind.

An important social rite of those days was the toilet papering of houses. The kids selected our house, on more than one occasion, which was clearly a sign of social status and popularity among the older high school crowd. I still have a photo of Bomba, Kathy, and me, playing among the white streamers, my brown hair hanging limply below my ears after a bad haircut, while Kathy sat cross-legged on the lawn, looking cool and confident.

One summer, we drove to Texas and, when we returned, Bomba was gone. She had died of a respiratory infection while in the care of our neighbors who buried her with the others out back. Somewhere in that yard, after all these years, is a monkey skeleton, the remains of my little monkey sister.

John, Kathy, Cousin Kim, and Martha play with Bomba.

CHAPTER 14

A Happy Family

"For health, and strength, and daily bread, we praise thy name oh, Lord."

We were a "together" family. We sang grace at the dinner table. On Sundays, all six of us piled into the our Dodge van and drove to the Unitarian Church, where it seemed each of us had our own spot to hang out in, with our own sets of friends. The church was a vibrant place, alive with people laughing and communing together—pulsating with endless political discussions and debates of the day. It was a time of happy renaissance for our family.

In the dappled light that fell on the grass beneath the pepperwood trees, I watched my sister leap high in the air, catching an errant Frisbee with the other teenagers romping on the church grounds. Laughter peeled through the air from across the patio where the grown-ups were drinking coffee during the social hour after the service.

For Kathy, more than any of us, this was her time and place—a time when she clicked with her friends, in the church youth group, and with the rest of the congregation in a perfect pitch. She blossomed with love, giving and receiving generous hugs to young and old. It was a rich period in her life and Sundays were the highlight of her week.

To me, my older siblings' youth group seemed like the be-all-and-end-all of coolness. I longed to be just like my sister and her friends and sit and listen to rock music while gazing at the black light posters in the teen lounge. But I had my own younger group for field trips and fellowship.

After the service and coffee hour, the kids' programs ended and our family got to work. We loaded up the recycling that the other congregants had brought, noisily tossing them into the back of our van.

Then we drove a short distance to the recycling center at the nearby university for more sorting and throwing into containers. This was great fun and a way for us to contribute to "The Ecology," as we referred to environmentalism at the time.

We were a together family, a working unit. We had a Cocker Spaniel.

So why did it all fall apart?

Grahams 1967: John, Helen, Jack,
Martha, Kathy, Charlie.

PART TWO

The Unraveling

CHAPTER 15

Signs Along the Way

Growing apart doesn't change the fact that for a long time we grew side by side; our roots will always be tangled. I'm glad for that.

~ Ally Condie, *Matched*

ᏋᏋ

I don't pretend to understand what happened to my sister. It is impossible *to* understand the reason for these things, after all. But there were signs, to be sure, well back into childhood.

I was ten and it was around Christmas time. I had just come home from a Bluebird meeting one afternoon. We had made Santa Claus candy jars, glass with a Santa hat, a felt face glued on top, and cotton balls for a beard. The jar was filled with red-and-white-striped hard candies.

I proudly placed my Santa jar on the dresser in our room and then watched in disbelief as Kathy snatched it up and smashed it to the floor, breaking it into pieces for no reason. I was shocked and cried, not so much from fear as from confusion, mystified. What had I done to her to deserve this?

Yet, in spite of these ripples on the surface, the years rolled on, mostly placid, carrying us along in their never-ending current. Kathy grew into a strong and beautiful girl with long, jet-black hair streaming down her back, a proud Tomboy who excelled in all manner of sports and leadership. Our family room shelves were crowded with the shining sports trophies she had earned. *Maybe someday I'll win a trophy for something*, I hoped to myself.

I continued to look up to her as I timidly crossed over the precipice from childhood into junior high, looking scrawny and awkward in my preadolescence, my nose a bit too large for my face, hiding my braces behind a tight-lipped half-smile in school pictures. We were on the cusp—on the verge of adolescence, the cracks and tension just starting to build.

Later, she was the one who had boyfriends coming around, who she would take under her wing. They even let me hang out with them sometimes as we listened to records together in the living room or walked up the street to the shopping center, a favorite haunt for bored teens.

I watched Kathy dancing in the social hall at our church under the oscillating lights of a dance globe. In white culottes, a puffy blue blouse, and white boots, she looked like a go-go girl, poised and in control, as her arms and legs swayed from side to side in time with the music and she tossed her dark hair carelessly behind her.

So that must be how it's done, I thought and, when I was brave enough to join the older kids on the dance floor, I followed her lead just like I had always done, imitating her moves, trying to look just as cool as my older sister.

ᏋᏋ

On a bright Saturday morning, I entered the kitchen in search of breakfast. Kathy was already up and raring to go. She was wearing sweat pants and a T-shirt and would soon be heading to a track event of the Girl's Athletic Association. She was juggling oranges up and down the length of her arms, seemingly effortlessly. First two, then she grabbed a third in mid-stream and, as they rolled down the length of her muscular arms, she caught and re-launched each one, in an automatic motion, as simple as brushing her teeth.

"Wow!" I couldn't help but exclaim. "When did you learn to do that?"

"Oh, it's easy! Want to give it a try?" Kathy stopped mid-stream and turned to me with a supportive smile.

"Well, okay." I picked up a couple of the smooth balls of fruit and tossed them from hand to hand. *So far so good.*

"Now throw them a little higher and I'll toss another in."

The higher part worked, at least, but I was never much good with round objects, be it softballs or fruit. In fact, the long distance softball throw was the only thing that held me back from receiving a Presidential Fitness Award in PE. Kathy had a multitude of these award patches sewn proudly onto her gym clothes.

When the third orange launched into the orbit, everything fell apart and the three bright orbs bounced onto the floor and rolled under the counter. "Can you show me again, Kathy?"

"Sorry, Marth. My ride's here. Got to go. Catch you later." She headed out the door, cheerfully whistling a pop tune.

I bent down, gathered up the oranges, and gave it a few more tries with the same results. Finally, I gathered up the fragrant, and now softer, plump balls and put them back in the fruit bowl. Oh well, at least these would be juicy now, I thought. But I couldn't help but wonder. Why couldn't it come easy for me too?

ഗ്ദ

It was those early teen years that turned out to be Kathy's best years—her golden time—but we didn't know how fleeting it all was. In later teenage years as her composure slowly crumbled, I witnessed her strength turn into hysteria, as her illness reared its awful head.

☙❧

When the morning alarm sounded, Kathy and I stirred in our twin beds and then rose, not wanting to be late for the walk to school with our friends. On the dresser mirror, she had taped a note with a smiling faced character as a reminder of what was to come.

"Glee Club today!"

Just the thought of that seemed to make her cheerful. Like me, she loved to sing and fool around before school with her friends and with Mr. Simms, one of her favorite teachers.

Yet in the scramble to get dressed, suddenly her mood changed.

"Who took my shoes?" she ranted, digging desperately through the closet. "God damn it to hell!"

These words, often directed at my mom, were turning into her favorite mantra as any order we had enjoyed in our life slowly began to fade away into nothing.

That Christmas, we were at a holiday party and Kathy was playing with a toddler on the floor. Suddenly, she became rough and, grabbing the little girl by the arms, swung her around in a semi-circle, back and forth. The child landed on the floor with a loud plop each time, but Kathy continued propelling her faster. The mother was there almost instantly, protectively snatching the child away. I smiled at her apologetically and sat quietly across from Kathy, hoping to calm her down with my presence, suddenly not feeling like a kid sister anymore.

A sense of despair started to gnaw away deep inside me. Now I knew that something was terribly wrong…

CHAPTER 16

The Dance

Find me where I lie.
My lips slide between and around your own.
Feel your body to be different than the self I have known.
Build me for my life.
~ KG

I watched my teenage sister spin and twirl around the living room, lifting her arms to the sky, in gestures of joy or twisted with conflict. She had a passion for modern dance, which she was learning in physical education class. She danced to the music from her collection of 45 records, which she piled high in a stack on the stereo—all of the classics that I still love. "Try to Love Somebody Right Now," "In the Year 2525," Janis Ian's "Society's Child," and more. The dancing was an outlet for the emotions swirling inside her that were begging for release.

When the time for Kathy's European tour arrived (probably around age fifteen) a travel program was selected and I tagged along to a meeting held somewhere in the canyons of Los Angeles. Looking back, I knew she had already started to slip away.

It could have felt like someone, or something pushed her off a cliff, to suddenly be apart from her family in a foreign land, but she did get joy out of the trip and made some friends. I was grateful that she experienced so much during those years, more than most kids might ever dream of.

In a black and white photo, I saw her walking down a boarding plank in front of a cruise ship off the isle of Corfu with her new friends, holding a notebook under her arm, slightly apart from the others, looking contemplative but content, at least on the outside.

Our summer European trips were "study travel" trips that opened up our lives and minds to the world, and Kathy eagerly drank in all of the adventures that the trip offered to her.

Years later, I sifted through her things, trying to unlock the mysteries of her mind. There were slides from her European trip, foreign bills and coins, and there was a postcard from Corfu, one of her favorite places. She loved to say, "The isle of Cor*fu*!" with enthusiasm and a fake Greek accent.

Kathy is on the right, disembarking in Corfu.

CHAPTER 17

Music is Our Muse

I think the music of today is my generation's statement to the ages. ~ KG

ഗ്ദ

Music was a vital part of our family life, weaving through the fabric of the times.

Time it was, and what a time it was.
It was a time of innocence, a time of confidences.
Long ago, it must be. I have a photograph.
Preserve your memories. They're all that's left you.
~ Paul Simon

More than anyone, Simon and Garfunkel's music and profound lyrics spoke to our whole family. We played their latest vinyl over and over again on the stereo, along with Bob Dylan; Carol King; Elton John; Peter, Paul, and Mary; Joni Mitchell; The Beatles; The Who; The Birds; and Crosby, Stills and Young. The record collection just kept on growing.

Our den, located midway between the bedrooms with doors on both sides, was transformed into a music listening zone. In this small room, we would sit quietly in the mornings after we got ready for school and listen to records. It was a peaceful, meditative time as we grooved to Simon and Garfunkel and laughed at Bill Cosby's routines. This was cutting-edge entertainment! And there was no better way to spend the afternoons than kicking back in the living room and looking at album covers, while the stereo serenaded us with poignant, moving lyrics.

Music was our touchstone. It marked the passage of time and our milestones. We never tired of listening to the songs of longing and pain, along with hope and optimism, love and struggle that paved the way in a time that was somehow simpler than today.

"Obla-di, Obla-da, life goes on, *BRA*!"

Kathy and her best friend blurted out this Beatles lyric while giggling hysterically—and later grooved to the music from *Hair* playing at the Aquarius Theatre in nearby Hollywood.

Harmony and understanding
Sympathy and trust abounding
No more falsehoods or derisions
Golden living dreams of visions
Mystic crystal revelation
And the mind's true liberation
Aquarius!
Aquarrrius!
(From the soundtrack of *Hair*)

As for me, I longed to be a part of the counterculture I saw around me, but I was not often allowed to go out with the older kids, who did not want their whiny kid sister hanging around. So, instead, I just quietly absorbed everything I could like a sponge. As the youngest family member, I was treated both specially and derisively—teased, yet somehow always protected beneath their warm wings. Within the walls of the family, my safe haven, I always knew who I was. We were The Grahams, forever and always.

CHAPTER 18

Run Over by the World

On the brink between childhood and adolescence, part of growing up for me meant getting glimpses of a dark world beyond the sanctity of my childhood. The Vietnam War dragged on. I became aware of the drug culture and of just how complicated everything was.

And then there was the car—and the day my childhood really came to an end…

ᏋᏋ

I knew I was craving attention that summer. I needed something that I couldn't explain, to be noticed, somehow, more than I had been, even though, on the outside, my actions said I wanted to go off on my own to rebel and find my own way.

They say that sometimes it is trauma that brings schizophrenia on, drawing it out of the dark recesses of the mind and thrusting it into everyday life. Suddenly, then, it is there, like a two-headed monster, never to retreat back into the cavernous reaches of the subconscious. It is awakened, a raw wound ripped open and exposed to the light. A trauma like that was visited on me but also left my sister as its casualty.

I remember that we got a new dishwasher installed that day. The summer had just started and we kids were just milling about with no direction yet. I walked out of the house that morning and headed up the street to hang out with my two not-so-nice girlfriends who smoked cigarettes and hung out with low riders. We would probably get stoned and sit on the couch or hang out in the mall. Even though I was really nothing like them—the thing was, it felt like freedom to me and so I set out up the street that day.

As I crossed the intersection of two quiet streets, I looked to my right. Far away and blurred by the summer heat, I saw a brownish car approaching. It was far away and not a threat to me. Ahead of me I saw my friend Cheryl coming to meet me half way in the middle between our homes. I crossed into her block.

I did not hear it coming. I did not see it coming. But suddenly I was violently struck in the back and thrust forward and down to the pavement. Then the only sensation was my body being crushed and rolled, crushed and rolled, over and over in a surreal span of time and space that seemed to go on forever. I knew what had happened. I thought for sure I would never survive. *I am being run over! I will be mangled! I will be paralyzed!*

But the animal instinct of survival grabbed hold of my very core in an instantaneous fight, saving my life. I felt a tire on my legs and pulled inward, compressing my body into a ball, using the tumbling skills I learned from gymnastics. And the horror went on. The car paused, the car continued. It dragged me beneath its metal frame and until I finally rolled out at the back. I smelled the filth of the street that had pressed against my flesh. I saw the sky above. I was still alive. I heard blood-curdling screams. Those were my screams. In shock, I somehow got off the ground and moved away from the metal monster that had just barreled into my life like a speeding bullet filled with horror.

"Cheryllll! Cheryll!

My primal screams were somehow transformed into words as I yelled out my friend's name at the top of my lungs.

Shock was a state I had never experienced before. It was like floating, somehow, and not being there. I looked down at my legs and saw my corduroy pants hanging in tattered shreds. I saw my blood from the road rash in patches all over my body. Stunned, I sat down on the curb. Cheryl stood and stared down at me in disbelief.

A man stopped his car. The two girls who had hit me—one fourteen, one fifteen, neither with a license, one "teaching" the other to drive, the blind leading the blind—were now trying to drive away to get their parents. The man stopped them and told them it was a crime to leave. He knelt down in front of me and asked me for my address. I gave him my phone number.

"No, honey. What's your *address*?"

I gave it to him and, before I knew it, my entire family was running down the street toward me. They were as horrified as I was. John, the eldest, knelt at my head and held my body in his arms.

It was then I heard Kathy's voice shaking with fear. "She's not going to make it." She was terrified at the sight of me lying there.

But I didn't end up mangled or paralyzed. When I was placed in the ambulance, I closed my eyes and said a silent prayer of thanks because I was still alive.

Mom climbed in and kept saying things she thought were reassuring above the sound of the siren as we sped along.

My injuries proved to be mostly superficial, although I was laid up in bed, my legs wrapped in bandages, like a civil war soldier, for a good part of the summer.

I had survived. I was whole.

But my sister Kathy was somehow not. For her, it was too much of a bad experience and trauma when she was already teetering on a precipice. And it foreshadowed more tough times ahead.

CHAPTER 19

Teenage Blues

Wake up, my love, beneath the mid-day sun.
Teenage blues.
Belittlement.
I don't know of that, no. ~ KG

Kathy Graham

Kathy 1969, Junior High

Even though her world may have been starting to crumble, Kathy still clung to the island of normalcy as best she could, as she continued to excel in sports and student government in junior high school.

Still it became harder and harder for her to conform to what she experienced as the regimentation of school and society.

Even though she was a star on the track team, a poem she wrote at the time conveyed the conflict and alienation that was brewing inside.

About PE

Damn you who stand behind your tree,
Clocking my every move.
Damn you who sit there behind your desk,
Smiling and smiling at me but you never touch me.
Damn you.
What if I didn't?
What if I didn't cross over that line?
Why, Kathy, what a great run,
Think of the time.
What if I stopped just short
Of the finish line?
Damn you and your time.

To make me stop, to make me go, to make me show you just how much I know.

Just wind me up and set me down,
Now determine, do I have enough worth to stay around?
KG

Kathy was a rebel and a non-conformer. She was a leader for a while in junior high and her classmates elected her to student government. But when it came time to enter the social jungle of high school, marching to the beat of a different drum didn't seem to work anymore. We had been raised as free thinkers but as time wore on, Kathy keenly felt the need to fit in, even as she fought to maintain her individuality.

Her poems were a refuge where she could let go of the conflict and alienation that she felt.

A cold room,
I come to it,
To sit in a programmed place and time,
To start and stop at the sound of a bell,
For as if I couldn't keep my cool,
I would surely die.
KG

With her quirky sense of humor, it was easy to make light of any serious situation and to be silly and have fun when life was getting too heavy.

Kathy was affectionate and playful with the people she cared about.

There are people I have come to know.
And like a quiet, internal glow,
They spark me,
And I am happy to see them again

She had a few poems published in the library's literary journal. I wish I better understood the secret meaning hidden between the lines.

Kicking a hair curler
down the hall,
Pretending to be very, very tall,
was once a plane,
but paper punchers are.
What do you do with a lid,
when you don't have a jar?

Tough and strong, Kathy also possessed an underlying tenderness as seen through the eyes of her little sister, me. She became tearful at the signs of tragedy—like when we watched the movies of our day such as *Love Story* on TV.

At a movie theatre packed with teens as well as preteens, Franco Zeffirelli's *Romeo and Juliet* was showing. Kathy was with her friends, and I was with mine. Our eyes met as we left the theater and, as I saw the tears streaming down her face, our hearts were joined, caught up in the moment of Shakespearean tragedy, coupled with teenage angst.

The emotional balance was easily tripped in those years, especially as drugs came onto the scene. Never one to use them herself, Kathy was quick to comfort friends in the midst of bad trips, carefully leading them to safety.

She was great at touch football, track and field, and softball, earning trophies in these and just about every other sport. I watched one day in awe as she flew across the football field, cherishing that strong image deep inside, somehow sensing it was ephemeral.

I followed in her footsteps when we both competed in a city-wide track meet where I finished in a surprising third place.

But it was not an easy path. Kathy was a young athlete just prior to the passage of Title IX in 1972, the first step in closing the gender gap in sports. When she was in junior high, girls were not as validated or encouraged in sports as in academics and other pursuits.

As I read an old scrap of her writing, I discovered she was actually going to try to be on the boy's cross-country track team in high school and she was apprehensive about taking this innovative step. She also was a pioneer because she took woodshop, which was probably unheard of for girls at the time.

On a tiny, undated scrap of paper was a note to a friend. I found it in a little bag with a ticket stub from the Eiffel Tower so I know she wrote it after she got back from Europe.

The fact that she had it, of course, meant it she never

sent it, like so many other notes of hers I would come to find.

Jan,

I love you, even though you are same sex. I guess that makes it pretty heavy, though you're weird, not me. You have a funny face and your feet are flat. And your books are too big. Jan, are you going to buy a big car? Do you like school? It's killing me, I don't want to die. Being the first female on cross-country won't be so easy, you know.

Why should I stop asking dumb questions? I'm scared! So. Do you feel a lot of pressure being on a same sex softball team when it already deviates from the traditional sex shit?

I know I talk too much, but I can't help it. Do you remember when I said we talked deeply and you didn't think so at all? I think you're just a deeper person by nature and it wasn't deep for you but it was for me and I appreciated it. I'm just crazy but...

The note was unfinished, the small, ripped scrap of paper fading into nothing.

She was already fading away, like those unfinished thoughts. Nonsensical and scattered, yet revealing much of her confusion about her sexual identity. But there was no second wave of feminism yet—no ride upon that nurturing crest of acceptance that I would later come to enjoy.

She was alone with her fears and self-doubt, at the same time that her illness began to surface, and it must have felt like the world was crashing down on her. It must have been so frightening for her. I remember when she first admitted what was happening.

"I have an illness."

She was sitting in the family room with just me and a trusted friend, but neither one of us knew what to say in response.

That was so hard and so brave. I just wish we could have been more understanding and that someone would have known what to do.

Of course, I wish I had been there for her more. But I was struggling to make my own way. We had different friends and interests and so our lives branched apart into parallel, yet separate, lives.

How could I help her when I did not understand what was happening to her?

ꕥꕥ

Kathy was faltering in school, hanging on by a thread. Angry and defiant, she seemed to be swimming upstream, fighting against all the currents of conventional wisdom and everything we had known.

I watched her fight against the establishment, but it seemed to be leading nowhere.

Disillusionment

Stand tall
Up against the wall
Bitter and sighting all pillars
"Burn the mother down!"
Turn the world around
Don't really know what I've found
Just playing the bitter clown

KG

Her emotional outbursts were increasing. Like the thunderheads of an impending storm, these were signs of a wild and rapid deterioration in self-control.

One Sunday afternoon after church, I heard Kathy release a string of obscenities outside the teen lounge. As I literally turned away, I thought to myself, *No, I won't be like her*. For the first time, I did not *want* to follow her lead. After all, conforming had advantages that I didn't want to give up. Good grades were rewarded and doing what you were supposed to do led to more freedoms in the end, since you could be trusted and left to your own devices.

In the meantime, Kathy continued to rebel. It was a battle she was losing as she lost control of her life, the reins slipping out of her hands. And, all the while, she was bursting at the seams, the creativity oozing from her pores. Her poetry and prose broke forth and took hold, clinging to wherever it fell—in math notebooks amid quadratic equations, crammed in the margins of biology homework, mixed in with song lyrics of the day—exquisite and simple poems about life, love, and heart-breaking loneliness. Poignant, irrepressible words scribbled onto napkins and envelopes—a statement of herself left behind for prosperity. She wrote poetry scraped from the tip of an iceberg of pain.

Cut through my skin
and into my heart
and let me bleed to death.

Loving hard and furiously, she wrote of the pains and struggles of relationships and their endings.

Silence
Your face says
much more
than all the words
spewed forth.
That's why I wish
that sometimes there'd
be days completely
silent.
Then I wouldn't have to
listen to
all your excuses.
KG

CHAPTER 20

Fighting Mode

As Unitarian kids, we enjoyed the benefits and risks of liberal, free thinking. Even though I was only twelve at the time and barely pubescent, I got to attend the "Sex Education Weekend" at our church, along with my older siblings, where we watched films and "rapped" about sexual issues openly—not in the propagandist way we had been shown in school health classes. At the church, information was presented honestly and we were encouraged to make up our own minds and make decisions with our parents.

But what we learned there did not translate so easily into real life.

"I could get an IUD. It's available at Planned Parenthood."

I listened as Kathy tried to persuade Mom and Dad one night as we sat around the dinner table during one of our "family council meetings."

But it was clear that our parents had already discussed this and made up their minds. As usual, it was Dad who conveyed the message in his gentle way, although I could tell, by the hard look and set jaw on Mom's face, that it was a decision that would not be undone.

"No, Kathy, we think that's not a good idea at this time."

Finally realizing that her pleas were futile, Kathy leaned her head sorrowfully upon Dad's shoulder, giving up the argument, another struggle lost.

More and more, Kathy and Helen clashed like oil and water in the age-old battle between teenage daughter and mother. One afternoon, their emotions exploded in a verbal and physical climax that had been building for years.

"You will not leave this house and represent this family dressed like that!"

It wasn't really about the clothes but about control, as my mother struggled in vain to control her terribly-out-of-control daughter.

"You can't take away my right to wear what I want and hang-out with who I want! You've tried to take away everything else!"

Kathy moved closer, struck Helen below the eye, and

then tossed the liquid from the glass she was holding onto the ceiling. As usual, I froze in fear as I watched the scene unfold before me. These outbursts were occurring more and more often and they were as unsettling as the occasional earthquakes that rumbled beneath our Southern California home.

No one was seriously hurt in this altercation. However, the next day, Helen declared that she needed to wear cover up to hide the bruise below her eye when she went to her substitute-teaching job.

Kathy was defiant, still in a fighting mode. "Martyr, martyr. You love to play the martyr!"

Then everyone went about their day as we always did. Maybe if we acted as if it never happened, would it all just go away?

CHAPTER 21

Leap of Faith

As the conflicts at home grew, I struggled to forge my own identity, finding comfort in religion and my friends.

Being brought up as a free range Unitarian, with little exposure to the bible, made me wonder what I might be missing—aside from the Lord's Prayer, which Mom had taught me by rote in a church program. So one of my friends would bring tattered copies of bible lessons, from her Sunday school, and we would huddle in the corner of the playground, pouring over them during recess.

I was in the sixth grade when my friend invited me to attend the Baptist Church where I inadvertently accepted Christ—or maybe it was meant to be. Anyway, as I sat next to the adult leader of the Girls Missionary Guild, she read a passage from the bible. My friend Marianne poked me with her elbow and whispered to me.

"You're supposed to repeat it!'

And so I did. Now I was saved.

I joined the Girls Missionary Guild and wore the blue cap and skirt. For a year, I attended the First Baptist Church and sang in the youth choir. I desperately attempted to bear witness to my family, explaining, exasperated, at the dinner table that they would burn in hell if they did not follow Christ.

My parents finally gave in to my begging and attended a service. At the end, I closed my eyes tightly and prayed that when I opened them, I would see them stand and walk up to the altar to accept Christ. As the strains of the congregants softly singing "…to cleanse my soul of one dark blot, oh Lamb of God, I come, I come…" broke through my reverie, I opened my eyes to see my parents still sitting in the pew, their faces set in hardened frowns.

I broke down in tears. I knew, in that moment, that my faith was broken beyond repair. After that, I stopped attending that church but latched on to the Jesus Freak Movement popular at the time. I went to Maranatha rock concerts and watched the kids raise their arms to the sky and sway to the rhythms of New-Age Christian rock.

On a warm summer's day, I was with a neighbor and her older sister as we headed down the coast to a beachside baptism. We followed a path down from a rocky bluff to the sandy cove where a hippie-like crowd was assembled, swaying in prayer as many lined up to wade into the white surf. We watched as the minister lowered the believers, one by one, into the sea and raised them up, dripping, exuberant, and renewed.

After an hour or so of witnessing this great spectacle of faith, we headed back to the car. Walking away from the cliffs, my eyes connected with a long-haired bearded man in his prime, looking much like Jesus himself, his face aglow with joy and smelling of salt water.

"Praise the Lord!" He held both arms up toward the sky in reverence.

"Praise the Lord!" I responded, feeling the vibe and wishing for more than a passing connection.

Within a year, I would no longer be a practicing Christian. Yet I came away from that time with something I would fall back on throughout my life—the power of prayer.

CHAPTER 22

The Beach

Siblings are often the targets of rage and violence. So, above all else, protect yourself. Do what you need to do even if that means removing yourself from the situation. ~ MGW

ᘓᘐᘓᘐ

I remember the incident, the breaking point, when everything changed forever. The scene took place at the beach with a mutual friend and our dog. I was fifteen and she was nearly seventeen. And the girl with the long, dark his hair was far away, on a path toward pain.

My relationship with my sister, nearly two years older than me, had changed. I saw her as aggressive and stubborn, increasingly hard to live with, but still a strong, yet confusing role model.

She used to want to take on the world, but lately she was becoming more and more disturbed, distant, and confused.

It was getting harder and harder for me to hang out with Kathy, but we still did things together, as we always had. One timeless activity for kids in Southern California was driving southward on the Pacific Coast Highway to one of the myriad of beaches, where we could spend the day body surfing and sunbathing. That day, our friend Barb had offered to drive us in her beloved old coup and we took our latest dog, a black and white mutt named Fergie, along.

Kathy was quiet on the drive and when we got to the beach, she promptly lay down on a towel on her stomach, not looking up or enjoying the vista. Another dog agitated Fergie. She started barking and struggled to run away.

"Kathy, I'm going to take Fergie to the car," Barb said decisively.

Kathy did not raise her head but clutched the leash in a tightened fist, lying in the sand, not speaking or yielding to us.

Barb finally extricated the leash, took the dog, rolled down the windows, and locked Fergie in the car, unprepared for what followed. For as she was walking back toward us on the beach, Kathy seemed to realize what had been done against her wishes. She was up like lightening, running headfirst toward Barb with a visible rage pushing her on. What her rage was really directed against, we couldn't see—but as I watched her fly at Barb and tackle her to the ground, it seemed to me that she was in an entirely different dimension, consumed by anger.

It was as if a switch had been turned on and her pent-up feelings were being narrowed into a line of attack.

Kathy threw her whole body weight against Barb, pushing her to the ground. Now she had her in a deadly headlock and, with horror and amazement, I watched as she systematically and determinedly brought her fists down again and again on Barb's temples.

"Give me the keys! Give me the keys!" Kathy yelled over and over, trying to gain control.

"No! No! I won't give you the keys to my car!" Barb struggled unsuccessfully to break out of the headlock vice.

I stood horrified, unable to believe what I was witnessing. I pulled at Kathy cautiously, fearing her rage like a fire. Finally, I separated the two, convincing them somehow that we should all go home. Stunned, the three of us walked back toward the parking lot but I was still shocked and upset.

"Go away from us! Don't walk with us! You're insane!" I would always regret speaking those words, hardly knowing where they came from.

That was when she hit me in the face, on the chin, I guess, but I all I really knew was that I was suddenly lying face down in the sand. What a strange scene it was. A woman on the beach saw the fighting and came running over to us. When she found out we were related, she exclaimed, "I can't believe you two are sisters!"

As Barb and I climbed into the car, with the dog and Kathy separated from us and heading back to the beach, I sat trembling and crying in the car. Barb put her arms around me and we sat still, for a moment, trying to calm our nerves. All I wanted was to get away. There was no talking the situation over then, so we left and drove home. Looking back now, I feel as though I abandoned my sister. After I described what happened to our parents. I guess they went to pick her up.

The next day, we walked down the street to see the psychiatrist who had a home office down the street. Kathy wouldn't answer Dr. Bradshaw's questions. In fact, the whole incident seemed to be cleared out of her memory, and she went on living like before, only now she communicated even less, ignoring me and the rest of the family.

A few nights later, when we were lying in our beds, I asked her a question that had been gnawing at me. She seemed so unaware of me, as if I wasn't there. She was oblivious to my confusion and fear of her. I wanted to know if she cared at all.

"Kathy, do you care how you affect me?"

"No."

So the answer came, plain and simple. She was living in her own world, removed from me and everyone else. For me, that was the beginning of an end, as I witnessed her sink farther and farther into her own world, her depression, and her developing illness.

CHAPTER 23

High School

As a teenager, when you are feeling the most vulnerable and self-conscious, just wanting to fit in, it is especially hard to deal with a sibling's mental health issues. It is hard to explain and hard for anyone else to understand. ~ MG

It was my turn to start high school. I had gotten some new clothes and even a boyfriend, who Barb had introduced me to. Everything seemed all right on the surface, almost too right—downright boring, in fact. Something didn't feel genuine. Maybe it was our liberal values not fitting in neatly into the white-bread neighborhood.

Moreover, the discord at home had made me feel ill at ease, as if I needed to find something new and positive in my life. I decided to make a change and enrolled in a new program, the School for Educational Alternatives or SEA, which was a magnet program located downtown.

Each day, a yellow school bus picked me and the other students up and wound its way through town, stopping at two other high schools before we reached Poly High, deep within the inner city.

SEA and Poly introduced us to a new and engaging world. It was one of the only high schools at this time to be completely fenced and walled in, like a fortress, to protect us from drive-by shootings that sometimes took place in the heart of Long Beach. Guards with walkie-talkies, who we affectionately called "The Henchman," checked our IDs as we entered the main gate. Looking up, the school mottos, "Enter to Learn, Go Forth to Serve" and "Forward Ever, Backward Never," emblazoned on faded copper, were oddly inspiring to me.

Within the fortress, our little school within a school was teeming with artists and creativity. Courses in marine ecology, photography, music, and art, as well as standard academics and lots of field trips and enriching group experiences made the trip across town well worth it and a welcome change as I began my new adventure.

I took up with an avant-garde crowd, hanging out in our school lounge or at Coleman's Soul Food Cafe next door, where we could imbue a whole other culture that most of us middle-class kids had never encountered. We congregated at the counter or in the leather booths, laughing and talking, while enjoying a hot lunch of collard greens, corn muffins, and other colorful fare washed down by cokes and coffee.

"Earth to Martha!"

Curt was dressed to the hilt as usual in a flamboyant pants suit. An applique of flaming red lips fashioned out of cloth hung upon his belt, positioned suggestively.

We all headed back to school. Still amazed by how different and freer everything was here, I must have spaced out.

"We're all going to the art gallery to see the new show! Join us?"

"Sure."

It felt great to be included in this motley crew. Every one of us was a unique player in a spectrum of diversity—kids from all kinds of backgrounds and subcultures. And every one of us was accepted unconditionally for who we were. In our school, we were safe from bullying. In our school, we were no longer misfits.

We passed through the iron gates and into our own world, an island hide-away within an urban jungle.

Accept that your loved one has an illness that is more frightening than you can imagine. Let them know that you still love them, even though they may seem like a totally different person. Although they may not acknowledge it, they need your support and understanding more than ever before. ~ MGW

ଓଓ

In the meantime, Kathy was struggling at our home school, barely hanging on by a thread. More and more, it was as if she'd turned into an entirely different person. Instead of the sister I used to look up to, she was becoming someone else, someone I hardly knew. One day, word got out that she had gotten down on her hands and knees, crawling down the high school halls. When I heard about this, I just wanted to disappear. It was as if I feared she would suddenly appear out of nowhere to embarrass and humiliate me. But, at the same time, I missed the sister she had always been to me. *Where did that person go?*

My nightmare continued when Kathy transferred to SEA too, attending intermittently.

One night, we were at a school meeting in someone's home. Kathy became wildly animated, standing up and gesturing with her arms, as she preached about intergenerational conflict and groups needing to come together. Her face and ear lobes turned bright red, and no one could get her to stop talking. Her outburst finally brought the meeting to a close.

Sitting cross-legged on the floor with my head on my

arms, I just wanted to sink down into the floorboards in embarrassment and despair. My best friend Marla pulled the hair back from my face, giving me a comforting smile.

This was another turning point, when I realized that I no longer wanted to be like my sister, when I knew that I wanted to be on a different path. I wanted more and more to be *nothing* like her, to be *totally different*. What I desperately longed for was a normal life. It was this realization that propelled my life in the opposite direction and away from my sister. Yet, as I would come to realize, there is no such thing as normal.

Things changed quickly after that. She plunged into a dark place, and the distance between us seemed to grow. Those two years between us were transforming into a huge, impenetrable gorge. As time went on, her behavior grew less and less socially acceptable, the outbursts becoming more frequent and upsetting to us all. My sister had completely lost any self-control. She no longer seemed to know how to behave. And I wanted to have less and less of any of it.

CHAPTER 24

Ways of Coping

Find out what it is you love to do and immerse yourself in it. Follow your bliss; pursue your own interests, no matter what. Don't let anything stand in your way. ~ MGW

ଔଔ

I started playing the piano at the age of thirteen, late to be sure, but at least it was my own choice, and my own predilection that drew me toward it. After all, the small upright had been sitting and gathering dust for as long as I could remember. My brother Charlie had taken lessons as a youngster but found that it was not his instrument. It was the guitar that would later call out to him and to my father and John, the eldest. Kathy would also take it up, singing the sad folk songs of the day, like "House of the Rising Sun," and other folk tunes, with a haunting poignancy.

"You take a stick of bamboo, you take a stick of bamboo, you take a stick of bamboo, you throw it in the water, oh, oh, Tanya."

As for me, the piano became my friend, a welcome escape. At first, the childish exercises and scales seemed annoying, but before long my fingers were soaring over the keys and my emotions spilled out through the Chopin waltzes and Mozart Sonatas, leaving me feeling satisfied and less empty inside. Sometimes, I wished could play waltzes all day long. I would continue to turn to the piano for comfort all of my life.

I also began to find relief and escape from my painful reality by smoking pot, clinging desperately to tiny bits of euphoria like straws or life rings I could grasp onto.

And then one day when I was around fifteen or sixteen, I found a check for $50 made out to the Transcendental Meditation Center that Dad had thoughtfully left for me. I'd always had a spiritual bent and I had become interested in TM. Mom drove me all the way downtown to the TM center.

As I entered the quiet room, the smell of spicy incense hung in the air and I placed some fruit on the altar below a picture the smiling Maharishi Mahesh. I was given my own mantra, a key to help unlock my inner world. This lifeline would truly help me throughout my life, allowing me to go inward and become centered, finding some inner peace amid the turmoil around me.

CHAPTER 25

A Dream and Sweet Sixteen—Not

One night, I dreamed that Kathy and I were in our bedroom. Her bed was against one wall, mine was against another, divided by a double-sided desk just like in real life.

I sat up in my bed and faced a bright, yellow light emanating from her side of the room. I saw her on her bed, bathed in the luminous glow. In my dream, I spoke to her.

"Kathy, are you there?"

"My body is here but my mind isn't."

Her answer drifted across to me through the yellow rays like a beam through fog.

I was so disturbed by this dream that I stayed home from school that day. I described it later in my humanities class and someone said yellow represents intelligence. It was as if her mind was leaving, before my very eyes.

On my sixteenth birthday, it all came to a head. It was a sweet sixteen that was never to be. Kathy had gotten out of control. She was wandering around neighborhoods and sleeping on people's lawns.

My parents fought, in anguish and despair, over what to do as I listened to their raised voices down the hall. She would disappear for days at a time and then refuse to talk to us when she returned home.

This especially pained me since we shared a room and because I wanted her to confide in me, still believing we would always be close. But all I got back was a deafening silence from her side of the room.

Finally, my parents needed to do *something*. That afternoon, they called the police, who came and took Kathy away to Juvenile Hall until the next course of action could be determined.

Afterward, I sat still in the living room and contemplated the silence and loss that hung heavy throughout the house. A concerned neighbor knocked on the door.

"Everything okay, neighbor?"

My mother explained what had happened in hushed tones.

Kathy spent the night in Juvenile Hall and then was transferred to a private hospital, the first of many to come.

Private Hospital

June 26, 1974: Went to Los Alamitos Ranch with SEA School (the School for Educational Alternatives) then out to eat pastrami sandwiches with Harriet, (a high school teacher) then back to the hospital.

June 28, 1974: Been at hospital all day. Tomorrow I have a pass to go to a Scottish thing with Harriet. The Pipes (family friends) are coming down Sunday. Got to get a pass somehow. Didn't go to school today, will go Monday. Slept most the morning, too much medication or something. Kissed Dan Hartman today under the shade of the slide on the grass at the hospital. Very nice—friendly.

June 29, Saturday: Went to Scottish fair in Santa Monica Jr. College with Harriet and her gang. Was fun, got a little sun burnt.

Sun, June 30: Went to Church. Walked around the block, back up and down to the recycling center, it's still going pretty good.

Mon. July 1: Group therapy. They got me—I can't let myself be wrong—because I guess I thought whatever I did it wasn't mine while living under Mom—this time I was very wrong and it's gonna hurt a little when my pride wall begins to crumble. While living under Mom, I was forced to do things I didn't believe in. Went to school today—nothing going on.

July 2 Tuesday: Went to school on the cross-town

streaker (bus), we went to court—I'm eating too much candy.

Wed. July 3: Who am I? No school today. I think I'm getting better. Reading The Warrior of the Wondrous Isles. *Went home for the fourth. Ate at Carl's Jr. for lunch. Listened to records. Then back to the hospital.*

July 5: Went to that Norwalk place. I think I'll transfer there.

July 6: Went to the foot of Baldy—Ice House Canyon. Just walking and talking with Dad. We stopped a few places on the way back. Dinner at Dinajos.

July 7: Feeling reluctant and slow about Metro (Norwalk Metropolitan State Hospital). Got Denise's address.

KG

CHAPTER 26

My Turn

You have a life and identity that is separate and unique from your sibling and you must go on with your life with or without them. ~ MGW

ℭℑℭℑ

In the midst of all the changes, the time for my European trip rolled around and we selected a program through the National Institute of Foreign Study. I would be traveling with a group of kids from a private Catholic school.

Typewritten letter:
January 3, 1974

Dear Martha,

The application blank and the catalog finally arrived this afternoon, and I am delighted with your choice of programs. I don't think you can fail to have a wonderful summer no matter which one you get. I rushed immediately down to the bank for a Cashier's Check, so that it would be cash in hand as soon as the letter arrived in Greenwich, though really my personal check should have been quite adequate since I have paid expenses for three other students. I even took the letter down to the main post office to get it off by the first possible mail. Now all we can do is wait for an answer and hope that these groups still have spaces available. Let me know as soon as you hear anything, please.

I am sure Mother has told you of my surprise trip to Egypt. Josh and Julie (her brother, known to us as "Uncle Billy," and his wife) *had to give it up in October because of the war between the Arabs and the Jews, but the cruise down the Nile is now possible again and he suggested that I join them. You know me well enough to realize that I could not pass up a chance like that so, after an exchange of cables to London, I made the reservation yesterday afternoon and paid for it. As trips go, it is not a very expensive trip, and I wanted Mother to go with me, but she declined the idea, feeling that she could not be so far from home right now. It relieved my mind when she phoned last night to say that you know where Kathy is, and that she is in good hands. I hope she can get regis-*

tered in school and settle down to do some good hard work so that she can graduate with her class and go to Alaska with me this summer.

Much love,

Grandmother

ଔଔ

Type written letter:

June 12, 1974

Dear Grandmother,

I'm very surprised to find I have a mere thirteen days left to prepare for my trip. I'm so excited, I don't know what to do first, but I think that eventually it will all get done and I'll be ready and waiting at Oakland Airport on the twenty-fifth.(My group is traveling all night by chartered bus to Oakland from Long Beach.)

I'm sorry that I haven't written you before, but everything has been active and confusing. Having Kathy in the hospital has been hard for all of us to accept and for a long time I couldn't seem to get my mind off her. I've also been busy with finals and finishing up all my classes. You might be happy to know I'm receiving nearly all A's, I got a B in trigonometry.

I want you to know how I feel about this wonderful gift you are giving me. This trip could have been at a better time. Being on my own (more or less) and being in a totally new country will give me something I've needed for a long time—a chance to think, relax, and sort things out. Besides that, I know I'll be seeing many beautiful and exciting places and meeting many people. I have four small guide books to the cities which I'll carry with me along with three phrase books in Spanish, Italian, and French.

Charlie and his girlfriend, Katie are insanely jealous and so are all my friends, but everyone's giving good advice about what to do and see.

I feel very lucky to have such a loving and generous grandmother (so grand!). I hope I'll have time to write to you many times while I'm traveling. I will telephone you before you leave. I'm looking forward to talking to you.

Love, Martha

P.S. I'm enclosing copies of the campus fact sheet and itinerary. I'm sorry I haven't written and sent them sooner.

By the time I left for Europe, Kathy's problems had proved overwhelming for my parents and she remained hospitalized, first in a private facility and then, eventually, in a youth ward at Norwalk State Hospital. During our weekly visits, I felt traumatized from seeing her there and just wished the bad dream would end. But now there was a bit of resolution to it all. If I said "my sister is in a mental hospital," it meant she was no longer here, she was away, removed from me and my life.

Still, I began my European journey with a heaviness

and sadness draped over me like a cloak. On our first stop in Richmond, England, while staying at a university, I clashed with my chaperone, a strict Catholic woman, because I wanted to go experience an English pub on our last night. Instead, I was forced to wait at the dorm while the others attended mass. I told her about my disappointment when the group returned from mass. Since I had been taught to speak my mind, I logically suggested she create a log that we could sign out on if we went on our own excursions.

This made Mrs. Ducote fly into a fury, her voice rising. "You promised me you wouldn't make any trouble on this trip. *Go to your room*!"

I ended up sobbing in my room, and then some older girls befriended me, brought me a cool washrag for my face, and helped me to get myself back together. The next day, I found a quiet place inside the chapel. Hidden in the dark in a pew, I let all my pain and loss pour out in wracking sobs.

The few letters that arrived from my family were like a tenuous line, stretching across the ocean, and brought some comfort and familiarity. In spite of the problems at home, life was going on the way it always did, and our family, although fractured, was still intact.

One day a letter arrived from Kathy. As the chaperone handed it to me, I ran to my room trembling with emotion as I clutched it to my chest.

Dear Martha, How's it going? I'm here the hospital. I feel that I've been making progress in talking to others about myself and what I feel. There's a lot of changes going on at home—Mom and Dad are getting it together so, Mom worries, I think, about not living up to Grandmother's expectations. But everything else is going well. I'm going to another hospital that's cheaper and more like an institution. There may be some harsh rules but I think I'll be able to be more of my own person with a lot of peer group orientation. SEA. (School for Educational Alternatives) needs sensitivity and self-awareness programs. I have no idea what career I'll find myself in in the future. I guess I have to get the school thing more together, that's what I'll be doing at this new place.

Well, you're probably at somewhat the same place, in that many things happening to you cause you to look at yourself. I hope you're very happy. Martha, really I care about you and the rest of the family. I hope you will surface well now cause everyone else is. I know the family seems all falling apart but that's not true now.

Anyway—what about you? Write soon, okay?

Much dear love,

Sister Mary Kathryn

The advice and care Kathy offered me in the midst of her own struggles touched me deeply. Newsy letters from my mother, infused with optimism, helped fill in the cracks of the homesickness I experienced.

July 9, 1974

Dearest Martha,

Today we got our first mail from you—both from London. One, the first, made us glow with shared joy. The second, detailing the problem with Mrs. Ducote, made us glow with pride! You were truly mature and courageous in a very difficult situation, and I know of few sixteen-year-olds who would have been able to handle themselves so well in such a painful situation.

Of course, we are most eager now to hear the next episode and are hopeful that some constructive solution has been found for an unfair personality conflict. But regardless, your courage in seeking an immediate and dignified solution to the problem shows you to be able to cope, with strength and poise, which makes us very proud indeed. If you learned no more than this on your trip to Europe, it might well be worthwhile.

But—gosh, you've learned so much more! Your first letter left us breathless—and Charles and Katie turned pea-green, annoyed you're seeing all they missed in their beloved England! If you manage to do that much in each country you visit, yours will surely be the richest trip of all!

Kathy giggled appreciatively about your trip to the Wimpy Bar. It brought her whole trip back to her—and she really needed the lift. She, Dad, and I went today to visit the teen program at Metropolitan Hospital, which actually offers more than the very expensive private hos-

pital in Long Beach. It's a good set up, with kids helping make the rules, but with much support and group interaction. The school even has a TV studio, where the kids make their own films, plus a sort of huge college-like campus that includes ball fields, basketball and tennis courts, snack bar, etc. Kathy met the kids and really warmed to the place. She plans to move there next Wednesday. It's really great that she is willing—even eager—to make the change, with a good grasp of her needs. Tomorrow she and Dad plan a long hike.

Since the apricots are canned, my next project is to clear out and re-paint the den before the Guerreros arrive from Texas with your furniture and themselves as house guests. But first I'll have to clean the garage to make way for the excess furniture. See what fun you're missing...

Love,

Mother

ಌಌ

Despite my dissimilar religious background, the churches we visited became strangely comforting places for me, especially Notre Dame Cathedral. I loved the huge upward expanses filled with strains of music and prayer. We even had an audience with the Pope in Rome and I was moved by all the pageantry as I watched him being carried in on upon a litter.

During the long bus and train rides through the country sides of rainy France and sunny Italy, I sat by myself and stared out the window, coming to terms with the new lonely reality of my life. I was truly on my own and she was not beside me.

It was a whirlwind month-long trip, encompassing six countries. I learned to proudly recite them in a litany: England, Belgium, Holland, France, Spain, and Italy. At the end of that trip, after seeing so much of the world and being on my own for the first time, I faced the brutal truth—I had a life of my own that I was meant to live, with or without my sister.

Flying back to America, our plane soared high above the North Pole and I saw the aurora borealis, dancing in swirling bands of color and glowing light, floating far below. Witnessing this spectacle of nature, I felt elated, moving from window seat to window seat throughout the plane to get a better view. Like an epiphany, I felt in awe of all the wonder and beauty of life. I carried this spiritual experience with me for a long time. But like any high, the letdown was hard as I returned to face the problems of our family, along with the challenges of adjusting to high school.

Grandmother had another gift waiting upon my return home. A beautiful Eastlake antique bedroom set that family friends had brought for me from Texas. The bed had a huge carved headboard and it had a special history, as she had been born in the bed. There was a matching marble-topped dresser and bedside table as well. Thinking back, I realize all this replaced the twin beds in the room that Kathy and I shared for so many years. They must have done this for me to ease the pain of memories that filled the room.

☙❧

In spite of their best efforts, our family nightmare dragged on with no end in sight. After the expense of a private hospital became overwhelming and my parents had to place a second mortgage on the house to afford it, Dad had found Kathy a teen program at Norwalk Metropolitan State Hospital. We would go to visit her there for our weekly family therapy sessions. Thorazine was the psychiatric drug of choice in those days and, when we saw her, she held her arms in a semicircle in a doll-like stance, drugged and submissive. It broke my heart and tore me to pieces. Wasn't there any other way?

Late one night, as I heard Dad come in after visiting Kathy at Norwalk, I sensed something was very wrong. As I entered the dining room, I saw him standing with blood all over his shirt, his face and nose swollen. She had punched him in a fit of rage. My heart broke to see my beloved father hurt like this. As he solemnly explained what had happened, Mom and I stood frozen in disbelief, trying to remain calm.

I went to bed that night, feeling like we were living

within a dark cloud of despair. Our lives had become a living hell, full of painful memories and feelings of loss, and I knew I needed to find a way out before it was too late. Or would my life become just like hers, no matter what?

CHAPTER 27

Out on My Own

Don't let your sibling's illness define your life. Live your life for you! ~ MGW

ຜ

The situation continued to be depressing and our home was stifling with an air of hopelessness. One day, I retreated to the privacy of my room and lay on the bed as a whirlpool of emotions swirled inside me.

I looked up to see my mother standing in the doorway. "You know, Martha, this is just what Kathy did!"

Okay, maybe it was true. Was I also headed for madness? Even if I was, it didn't help to be treated like I was.

My relationship with Mom had become more and more strained and confusing.

One night at the dinner table she declared, in a resentful tone directed to my father, "Either Martha leaves, or I leave."

A stunned and awkward silence followed, gripping the air like a curtain had been dropped around the table between my brother, father, her, and me.

The thing was, Mom didn't really mean it. She and Dad were heartbroken over Kathy's illness, and they were struggling to deal with it as much as I was. Still, I was shocked since I had done nothing to cause this unexpected outburst. I know now that she was hurting and resentful of Kathy and the disintegration of our family, and she easily transferred those emotions to me through flare-ups filled with mixed messages.

But I was drowning in a sea of ambiguity.

After transferring to SEA school on the other side of town and having to take a long bus ride there daily, my social life had slowed to a standstill because my friends were not nearby. Mom would not allow me to have a boy "alone" in my room, although there was no said boy to be had. Left in the solitude of my room with only my loneliness and painful memories, I felt swallowed up by the same despair that had destroyed my sister. I could not reconcile myself to her being in a mental ward, although my mother claimed the state hospital provided "the best possible care," and my parents seemed to accept the drugs—which sometimes caused hallucinations—along with the "therapy" imposed on her, to be the best course of action.

The more I thought about it, the more keenly I felt that I could easily follow the same path, something I truly did not want. And now my own mother seemed to be inviting me to leave.

When I was sixteen, almost seventeen, I could bear it no longer and felt bitter toward the world. One day, I found a note in my message box at school, asking if I would be interested in a new living environment with two girls who were also having problems at home. While I declined at first, the latest blow-ups at home led me to reconsider and I finally accepted the invitation.

We found a small house in a part of town not far from school with enough space for the three of us. The owner ran a beauty shop alongside the house, seeing her clients in the afternoons. So a large red and white sign on the front lawn read, "Florence's House of Beauty."

This landmark was easy to find and the source of many off-color jokes about houses of ill repute, etc. But the wildest thing that was ever to happen there was when young people were drawn in for weekend parties in our living room like moths to the flame. There were live bands, and beer bottles were strewn across the living room in the mornings, following these soirees.

After about six months of this, I just wanted to be alone, away from the harshness and noise of the world. A teacher at school helped me to procure a small studio apartment for $90 a month. I was earning $50 a week through a high school work-study program, transcribing recordings for the Folk Life Center at the university. With an occasional $20 spot thrown in from my dad—in 1975, it was just enough to get by.

My new little studio was one of four in the building. A sunny garden separated it from the large Victorian house in front. Even though it was located in a seedy part of town, all in all, it was a good fit for me, since I could walk to school. One of my high school friends ended up renting one of the other units. Mine was located up a narrow flight of stairs.

After school, I bounded up the cave-like entry way, placing my keys on the marble entry table Grandmother had given me and entered my own world. There was even a tiny balcony, where I could look out at the world. I pulled down the Murphy bed at night to sleep and had a little Calico cat who I named Serendipity to keep me company. My friends thought this arrangement, so different from most, was totally cool.

In the afternoons, I walked toward the ocean and the downtown area, and into a towering ivory white building, where the Folk Life Center rented a small office. Here I would type transcripts from recordings of people's life stories for my weekly stipend of $50. I enjoyed typing and turning off my brain for a couple of hours, then logged off and walked back to my studio.

On my way home one day, I noticed a lot of activity going on in a small building that looked like a storefront just down the street from my place. Hippie-like people were unloading goods and walking in and out. Stepping inside, I saw shelves and coolers filled with organic food, some that were strange and foreign to me. Kefir yogurt drinks and white tubs of Tofu, along with grainy chips, chunks of shrink wrapped cheese, and colorful fresh vegetables packed the aisles.

A young woman with short hair and round spectacles peered at me curiously. "Hi, are you a new member here?"

"A member? Of what?" Whatever it was, I knew I wanted to be a part of it.

"This is the Food Co-op. Welcome aboard."

And so I eagerly joined in with the colorful tribe—ladies in flowing skirts and peasant blouses and long-haired young men, one in particular…

 cscs

I was infatuated from the first moment I met Tom. He was friendly and easy-going as he showed me how to work a shift at the counter and help unload the incoming produce. With his clogs and painter pants, he seemed very worldly to me, his twenty-two years made me look up to him and our budding relationship helped me gain entry into this slightly older crowd.

At the co-op, I traded time working for the privilege of buying affordable, healthy food. I could buy meager amounts of groceries here while socializing with cool people. Before, I was living hand to mouth—frequently eating at Coleman's and other diners, frugally bringing home the left-overs boxed up for another meal. But after joining the co-op, I learned to steam carrots, make brown rice and vegetables, and grate white cheese on top. I could actually *cook* in my own little kitchen.

The co-op was also a needed social outlet. There were occasional dances on the weekends with blue-grass bands and people of all ages to hang-out with, right there in my own neighborhood. My world had brightened. I finally started to feel happy.

Yet there were still drawbacks to living off by myself.

Although I was removed from it, my relationship with my family was still troubling. In spite of what she had said to me back at the dinner table on that fateful night, my mother began to write me scathing letters, criticizing my decision to leave home, implying that I had abandoned her.

Soon, Grandmother joined in, sending me a letter that drove me farther into despair.

Dear Martha,

You have a brilliant mind and a beautiful body but still you are not happy.

You may say, as some have, that I didn't ask to be born into this world. Well, your parents didn't exactly plan for your arrival either. You nearly ruined your mother's health and caused your father to have a vasectomy to avoid any future such accidents. But they loved you and welcomed you and gave you a good life.

Your parents already lost one daughter to illness. Of course, we should pity instead of blame her. But to lose a healthy daughter as well must have been more than they could bear.

This cruel letter, sent by my own grandmother, someone who had always been so kind, devastated me. The heartless missive cut like a dagger, only adding to the misery I was experiencing, as I tried to build my own life.

I stuffed the letter into my pocket and carried it with me for days, hoping to be able to share it with someone, but would anyone understand? I fingered the letter in my pocket as I sat in class. It burned a virtual hole through me and the emptiness grew, threatening to swallow me up.

"Can I show you something?"

Brad, who was one of my SEA school friends, and I were sitting in Coleman's Soul Food during lunch.

I read the letter to him and told him I felt like tearing it up. I was full of rage.

"Tear it up if it makes you feel better." Brad understood. He had his own troubles with an alcoholic father at home.

In the end, I kept the letter and finally wrote back to Grandmother, defending myself, trying to soothe the hurt, but we would never again experience the closeness we once had.

ꕥ

One winter's night, I was sitting alone, cross-legged, staring soulfully into a candle flame in my sparse studio. Only it was not a spiritual meditation—it was because I neglected to pay my electric bill.

That was one of the many lessons I learned during those times. They were tough experiences that I would not recommend to anyone, yet the experience of living alone did make me more in touch with myself and stronger.

Thoughts of Kathy still troubled me in the quiet of the studio as I agonized about her fate and my own. Waking up in the darkness one night, I sat bolt upright in my Murphy bed, feeling totally alone and in a void, as if there was absolutely no one else in the world beside me. The lessons of solitude came hard. Later in my adult years, I would never choose to live alone again.

ꕥ

Your older siblings foreshadow your life, laying out expectations in front of you and footsteps to follow like some kind of rising obstacle course. ~ MGW

ઌઌ

"Please take this class attendance to the office, Kathy—I mean, Martha."

My English teacher made the slip up that I had heard throughout my school years. I could see that he regretted saying it, since he was aware of the situation going on in our family.

"No problem." I grabbed the form and headed out the door. The mention of her name was starting to hurt less and was less embarrassing. It was not the first time I was mistaken for my older sibling and I knew it would not be the last. That was simply an occupational hazard of being the youngest child.

I looked to my teachers in the alternative school for guidance, still yearning for parental figures, even though I still saw my parents frequently.

My English teacher, Colin Campbell, became my protector. He read my journal and poetry and encouraged me to write, responding to my lonely rants.

January 1975

So many simple songs

The empty melodies and lyrics

Fall still upon my ear.
I am entranced by the sounds
Kathy was real tonight. It's true. She knows what she thinks, wants and needs.
We always tell her what she thinks
when we don't really know.
She is better. A lot better,
in comparison to several months ago.
I projected myself on her.
That I didn't like the hospital.
That I didn't like where she was coming from.
Kathy, Kathy, Kathy. Who is she really?
Have I forgotten her?
Fire and idol of my childhood?
Have I really freed myself from her?
No. She's inside me. Always.
Maybe when I lose control of myself,
my life goes wild, and I can't see why,
maybe it's that memory stirring in me.
A lost part of me. Kathy.
She will get well.
MGW

My journals were very intimate, almost too personal to share.

But it was comforting to feel like I was being heard by someone who cared enough to answer back.

January 21, 1975

Dear, dear Martha. I am frustrated. I would that I could respond to your journal, but I do not know if I can. Here goes.

Life consists of movements. It has its ups and downs, securities and insecurities, its areas of stability and of instability. Life is endangered if limits are not set on the extremes. We need social encounters, and we need time alone. We need a sense of personal worth, and a sense for self-examination. As we long for social acceptance, so must we give acceptance to others; as we look critically at others, so are we looked at critically. In all things, we must avoid excess.

You have to make a choice: am I going to survive, or am I going to thrive? If the latter, you have to seize hold of both ups, and downs, and hold on, and then wield what you can.

In his classroom, the sunlight poured in like yellow butter through the open windows, as we sat on the pine desks, and he shared half his sandwich and coffee with me during lunch. We discussed my journal and our lives like lifelong friends.

"You know Martha, if you *could,* someday you might want to write a book about your family."

Then the bell rang and I headed out the door. As if I could ever put any of this down on paper! It just seemed like such a Herculean task.

ઙઙ

Later that day as I sat on a bench across from the school, waiting to take the bus to my little studio, I saw Colin standing like a sentry in front of the school. His unfaltering gaze was directed across the flowing traffic, looking directly at me. He maintained eye contact with me until I boarded the bus, somehow knowing how I could carry his comforting concern with me throughout the weekend. He knew my despair and he made sure I survived it.

CHAPTER 28

Back to Norwalk

In spite of my own struggles, my mind always seemed to wander back to Kathy. What would happen to her? How could I help? *Could I?* As I agonized about what would happen to her, my own experiences as a high school student living on my own helped anchor me firmly in reality.

Just as I was adjusting to my independence, Kathy was also settling into a routine. She attended school at Norwalk State Hospital and gained access to the grounds and passes for home visits. Once I got my license, they allowed me to pick her up from Norwalk for a visit.

I was still living with two other teenaged girls at "Florence's House of Beauty" in downtown Long Beach when I brought her back to stay the night, but Kathy pushed the envelope by not taking her meds. Soon she slid into a psychotic meltdown, like hitting a brick wall of reality and then crumbled to bits. She lay curled up on my bed unable to communicate.

She turned her head toward the wall and pressed her hands against her face, crying silently in utter despair, facing demons I couldn't see.

I ran my hand down her back, trying to comfort her, but she was in an emotional abyss that I couldn't begin to reach. So a friend and I drove her back to Norwalk and checked her back in.

I felt the sadness and helplessness return as my friend embraced me in a long hug. There was nothing else that I could do to help my sister. But I so wished that I could!

CHAPTER 29

The Fear Factor

Don't expect the world to understand, but remember you are not alone. ~ MGW

ഗ്ദ

There are roughly 10,000 genetically related illnesses lurking around [http://library.thinkquest.org] or something like that. Cancer, Alzheimer's, Down Syndrome, Hemophilia, Muscular Dystrophy—to name a few.

But none are stigmatized in the same way as mental illness.

"So sorry to hear about your family member's cancer," is a socially acceptable comment, while "So sorry about your sister's schizophrenia" usually is not.

Back in the 1970s, this was a subject which was rarely broached. And so I kept it a secret most of the time. How could I explain? Who would understand? When I did open up occasionally, releasing a flood of emotions, I usually wished I hadn't. Most kids just didn't get it—it was too foreign, too far removed from their own life experiences. As I struggled to understand my sister's diagnosis, I found very little tolerance or acceptance of mental illness as word got out around the school.

"It's a *hereditary* disease!" I heard an acquaintance say in a hushed tone as I made my way across the quad, further stigmatizing and isolating me.

Encounters like these only reinforced the sinking feeling, that I was doomed to a similar fate, as I struggled under the weight of my own depression. I never realized that other kids might be experiencing the same thing in their families as they watched their sibling or parent's transformation into a stranger they no longer knew.

ᏋᏕᏋᏕ

Schizophrenia: A severe psychiatric disorder with symptoms of emotional instability, detachment from reality, and withdrawal into the self. ~ Encarta Dictionary

Dad had just relayed to me Kathy's dismal sounding diagnosis of paranoid schizophrenia declared by Dr. Bradshaw. I went to the library and looked up the definition, reading it over and over, and still not understanding it. If only someone would have explained it to me and told us what it would mean to us as a family. How we could cope, what we should expect, and what we could try to do to help.

After all, mental illness was not a death sentence. Many people had learned to live with it. And like any other serious disease, it must be treated, dealt with, and discussed.

Years later, I took my daughter to see Mariel Hemingway at a book signing for her cookbook. As she started speaking, I felt a real connection with her life that closely paralleled mine. I had never heard anyone talk about what I experienced as a teenager—the terrible fear of losing my mind, almost knowing that it would happen, just like my older sister.

I was touched as I listened to her speak of her loss, not only of her sister but many family members to mental illness. She inspired me with her bravery and honesty in revealing the past and how she grew past the fear and pain, protecting herself through healthy eating and living. She also dealt with the specter of cancer in her family, caring for her mother until, like me, she left home at the age of sixteen.

I felt tremendous empathy for her. Especially since the world seemed to want to eternally connect her to the sad demise of her famous grandfather, even though he died before she was even born. But Mariel Hemingway had left this tragic legacy behind in history where it belongs. She didn't let family tragedies of the past define her present, choosing instead to create her own legacy, in her own right.

In this respect, I could so relate with her struggle for independence. I had sought to recreate a life for myself separate from my family, as we all must do on some level. It was that Mariel Hemingway, like my own reinvented self, that I celebrated and admired.

CHAPTER 30

Hamburgers and Milkshakes—
The State Hospital Circuit

"Martha, bring me a hamburger and a chocolate shake."

It had been a couple of years since I graduated from High School, with honors, proudly attending Grad Night at Disneyland with Tom from the food co-op as my date.

Kathy was back at Norwalk again.

I had called her on the pay phone in the hallway and then waited about ten minutes for someone to find her. "Okay, Kathy, see you soon."

She seemed happy to see me when I got there but immediately focused on the greasy and creamy treats I proffered. She was becoming more and more fixated on eating and drinking soda that added to her ever-expanding girth. She also requested cigarettes so I had bought one or two packs of a cheap brand and then presented them to her guiltily.

It was a stark scene in the state hospital. Most of the patients hung out in a large lounge area with big windows looking out over the grounds. They sat slumped in the oversized Naugahyde chairs with huge sloping metal armrests or rocked back and forth in comforting rhythms. Some played ping-pong. The nurses distributed meds several times a day, in paper cups, from the nurses' window. It was drab and sad and, when I was there, I felt like those gray walls were absorbing me, as if I belonged there, too.

I looked at my sister as she devoured her hamburger, reflecting on the divergent course our lives had taken. *It can't get much worse*, I thought to myself. I wished I could transport her away from the starkness of this institution. But I had my own struggles as I tried to make a living during a break from college. I was having an especially bad day after losing my job. I had a sunburn.

As I tried to start a conversation, Kathy suddenly rejected me.

"Whore!"

The word stung like a blow as she stormed away from where I was sitting in one of the huge Naugahyde chairs in the ward.

She saw me as snobby because I had my own car and

freedoms that she had lost, even though *she* was the older sister, not me. Suddenly I broke down, the pressures of my lousy day giving way to a torrent of tears.

I felt someone's arm on my shoulders. Looking up, I saw the kind face of a young woman comforting me. I stammered, "T—Thank you," and realized she was a patient.

"It's all right. You just looked so red," she said kindly.

Kathy came cautiously back over to see if I was okay and, suddenly, life seemed bearable again.

ଓଌଓଌ

After another visit at Norwalk, I was escorted into a small office to meet with Nick, Kathy's latest counselor. She had had lots of these characters in her life, some helpful and caring, including one who was blind who told me that she was a survivor with a lot of inner strength like he must have had.

But the job had a high turnover and, on this day, it was her new counselor, Nick, who wanted to talk to me. He had black, tightly curled hair and a mustache and was young and clearly frustrated. *Must be new here...* I thought to myself.

Nick closed the door hard and sat down at his desk, his chair scrapping on the linoleum floor as he swiveled toward me provocatively, rolling forward until he was directly in front of me. I could sense his hostility even before he spoke, leaning toward me, almost in my face.

"You have ruined my therapy with your sister!" he announced, his face turning an angry shade of red as he struggled to maintain his self-control.

What is his problem? I thought. I knew, that because I had taken a Women's Studies course at Cal State Long Beach called Women and Psychiatry, I had talked with Kathy about her rights as a patient. *So that must be what this is about.*

"I just took her to a concert and spent some time with her. She is my sister, after all."

"Well, your sister needs to shave her legs and act like a lady!"

He was angry but my anger rose to match his. I had heard enough, and it was time to go. The last thing I wanted was to get into an argument with a male chauvinist.

"Bullshit," I muttered under my breath. I don't know if he heard me as I stormed out the door.

Many ups and downs followed, but Kathy finally left Norwalk State Hospital. She learned they would transfer her to another facility on request. So began her sojourn—Camarillo, Patton, the whole gamut of state hospitals in California, followed by many moves from one board and care to another.

After the Thorazine, there was a litany of other psychiatric drugs. Risperdal, Haldol, Clozapine…there were others I was not aware of because Kathy liked to keep her drugs and medical history hidden from her family. It was one thing she could control because of patient confidentiality laws.

One summer, I went to visit her at Camarillo State Hospital during a road trip to Oregon with a friend. I was reading *Woman on the Edge of Time* by Marge Piercy and the story line, about a woman who was hospitalized in a mental ward, seemed to eerily parallel reality as we drove onto the sprawling grounds.

Many of the old state hospitals had extensive lawns and established shade trees, creating a feeling almost like that of a college campus.

In fact, I later learned that the grounds of Camarillo were converted into a university. Back then, it was a dreary expanse of lawn and tall, derelict buildings, disguising the human drama within their gray walls.

Yet at times, the hospital grounds were quiet and strangely serene. Shade tree canopies hung over soft grass.

When given the luxury of a grounds pass, it was here, outside and in the open air, where she could find a moment of peace and enjoy a smoke as we sat and talked.

"You want a cigarette, Martha? Come on, smoke with me."

Kathy wanted to share with me one of her few pleasures, her indulgence, her tobacco fix.

I was tempted, as I thought back to our times up in

the old sappy back yard tree and my first puff of cigarette smoke that nearly suffocated me.

"No thanks, Kathy."

CHAPTER 31

The Red Barn

Many people befriended Kathy during the course of her illness, especially as a teenager. A teacher from our school and family friends took her in. She went to live with my aunt in Bakersfield who empathized with her because of her own struggles with manic depression. But eventually, things would fall through and Kathy would end up back in the hospital or in board and care.

One couple from our church, Clark and Joanne, became involved and Kathy often stayed with them. They never had a daughter and Clark especially seemed to want to rescue Kathy from her illness and talked about writing a book about her.

I still wanted desperately to help her. Around 1978, I

was living in a rented old two-story house with a large front porch next to a park. It had a red and white frame and it became known as the Red Barn to my housemates and me.

One day, Clark picked Kathy up from the state hospital and delivered her to me at the Red Barn "on a pass." As fate and politics would have it, this was when our then Governor Ronald Reagan chose to turn loose patients from the state hospitals out on the streets in a dispassionate attempt to fatten the state budget. But I didn't know this at first. I was just trying to reconnect, to somehow help pull her out of the institutionalized fog and stupor of drugs and illness that had held her back.

We were sitting in the dining nook of the old house and the sunlight filtered in through the curtains as I brought some scrambled eggs and potatoes to the table. Kathy reached up and placed her hand on my leg as if grasping at reality, afraid that I might fade away. Her eyes traveled up to my face and she gazed at me searchingly, wondering if this place and even her sister were real. After so much silence since she arrived, she finally spoke.

"I wish the voices would stop."

"What do the voices say, Kathy?"

"They tell me that I am bad."

"But you're not. I think you may need to take your meds now."

"In a while. Is there any hope for me, Martha?"

Suddenly, all the resentment I had ever held toward her rushed away and I was filled to the brim with overwhelming love and pity. All I wanted was to be able to help her somehow, to do something to end the tortured mess that she had had to endure. It was a deep-seated need that I would carry with me for many years to come.

"There's always hope, Kath."

I got her to eat something and then she went outside for a smoke. But soon my optimistic plans faded as our visit began to fall apart.

I was working the swing shift at an aerospace plant. We would spend the day together before I had to leave for work around three in the afternoon, but the days began to crumble into chaos as Kathy stopped taking her meds. Her ability to communicate and function quickly deteriorated before my eyes.

"It's time to take your meds, Kathy. Where are your meds?"

She would not answer me and I couldn't find them among her things. I watched as she wandered the rooms downstairs, cocking her head to the side and pointing to her ear.

"Telephone?" she crooned.

I could see that she was totally out of control and hallucinating. Later, I found her shuffling down the street in her socks. Somehow, I convinced her to come back inside the house.

It was then that Clark informed me over the phone

that the "pass" was for good and that she could not return to the hospital.

Not knowing what to do, I called Dr. Bradshaw who prescribed an anti-psychotic drug of some kind. He suggested I crush it up and put it in her food. Desperate, I did so and she quickly transformed back into a sweet and cooperative person, which allowed me to leave for work.

My landlord was not understanding about the situation, however, and he gave me a week to get her out. I found a board and care home, a former apartment complex called Chezbonne, where the understanding director agreed to take her in. She stayed there for several weeks, even though no money was paid. Eventually, even that lovely lady could take no more and, when I went to visit, she told me Kathy was relieving herself on the floor, among other things, and that she would have to leave.

At this point, my parents stepped back in and had her reclassified as a ward of the state, allowing her to return to the system. I continued working and visited her back at the state hospital when I could.

When I was enrolled at the local university and lived in an off-campus dorm, she showed up one night, looking for me and walked into someone else's room, exclaiming about all the nice things they had, then she ran off.

The resident assistant found me and I called Clark. We found Kathy and took her back to the hospital—always back to the hospital. The students, although puzzled, were nice enough not to say anything to me about it the next day. I called the hospital a few days later to check in with her.

"Hi, Kathy, how are things going?"

I could hear noise in the background. She cleared her throat but didn't answer.

"Are you going to group therapy there?"

Silence. This phone call seemed pointless—it was just my weekly act of contrition. I'd wait a while longer and then end it.

"Martha, did you know your father is a murderer?"

I hung up the phone.

CHAPTER 32

Why Do I Love You?

It's okay and normal to feel resentment, even hatred toward your sibling. You may wish to forget your sibling, and maybe you will for a while, but unlike friendships, it's not a relationship that you can simply walk away from. Your sibling is ingrained upon your very being. Your life will go on and things will get better but their memory and impact on you can never be erased. ~ MGW

❧❧

My sister caused me much pain. Until I was finally on my own, the ups and downs of her illness and the drama of her life played out before me seemed to define my existence. And later, even while caught up in living my own life, the thoughts of her followed me like a shadow.

What had she ever done for me? Why couldn't I break free and just forget her?

Like others who had witnessed the promise of their siblings' lives stolen by mental illness, I had to wonder why. Why had this happened to her and our family? Why her and not me? It is our own brand of survivor syndrome. How could my life seem so sweetly beautiful at times when hers had been so miserable? Why was I was free to go on and live a full life while her life had been changed forever? I was plagued by persistent what-ifs. Couldn't I have done more to help? Could I do even more for her now? I had watched her settle into a routine of hospitalizations and medication that managed her symptoms and defined her days. Her simple pleasures were now smoking and maybe a daily walk to the local market to buy a coke.

Eventually, I learned to accept this new reality, just as she had, by realizing that, even though her life was very different from mine, it was still a tolerable life, it was *her* life. She was still my sister and I was grateful she was still around.

ꕥꕥ

"Maartha, this is your sissster." Kathy drew out her

words with an aristocratic English accent. She had been in the psychiatric ward for a few days, but was now back at her board and care. Her collect call to me had come as a surprise.

"How's your week going, Kathy?"

"Very well, indeed. Are you staying out of prison?"

I tried to laugh this off. "Yeah, well I hope so!"

"Maartha, I would like you to bring me some Wrigley's gum and Squirt soda and take me for a drive tomorrow."

"I'll think about that, Kathy. But I have to go to work tomorrow."

"A delicate thing like you shouldn't have to worry about a job."

"Well, the world doesn't owe me a living, so I have to. Don't worry about that, okay?"

"Just make sure you don't get arrested and incarcerated for twenty years."

I laughed again. "I'll do my best. Good-bye. Love you."

"Love you too, little *sissster*."

ဗ

Dad and I drove through the labyrinth of freeways and exited into one of the back-to-back cities that made up the urban patchwork of Los Angeles. A few turns and we were on a street with sidewalks and modest homes with green lawns. The people here didn't have much money but took good care of what they have.

We pulled up to the curb of a stucco house and followed a concrete walkway up the lawn to the brick porch.

Yolanda, a very vocal resident called out, "KATHY, YOUR SISTER IS HERE!"

Kathy emerged. It looked like she had gained about fifteen pounds. Her leather purse was slung across her body and her dark hair fell in limp strands around her face, her cheeks hollow without her dentures.

"Martha!"

She threw her arms around me in a tight embrace, not wanting to let go.

We drove to a local coffee shop where Kathy ordered all her favorites: a hamburger and fries, a coke, and then buttermilk. She had an insatiable thirst. Even though she took a shuttle to a day program several times a week, it was a treat for her to get out for a bit. When we returned, I walked her into the tidy little living room with its plastic covered couch and an oriental carved coffee table. Kathy proudly showed me the bedroom she shared with two other girls and the peaceful backyard shaded with fruit trees where she went to smoke.

I was glad that she was here and that she was no longer stuck in the state hospital. As I looked around and appreciated the simple comforts she enjoyed, I thought again about how different our lives had become.

In many respects, her life was easier than mine.

There was money for her needs and people to take care of her. I was still jumping from job to job, lay-off to lay-off, my relationships seeming to stop as quickly as they started. Still I knew what she lacked was the one thing I had worked for and treasured—freedom.

CHAPTER 33

What the Past Reveals

Don't waste your energy by trying to lay the blame for your sibling's illness. It's not anyone's fault. ~ MGW

ɞɞ

It was my interest in genealogy that had uncovered it. As I looked over a long, painstakingly drawn family tree that my great uncle had made, I saw it—a small note above my maternal grandparents' names that read "second cousins" and then earlier, the same notation above other ancestors in the family line.

Overturning this stone gave me pause. Was it this twisted genetic mix that had led to Kathy's illness? *How could they have done that to us?* Suddenly, I wanted to blame my grandparents, including the grandfather I had never known. Overcome with an irrational anger, I finally put aside the family tree and closed the computer chart I had been creating, not to revisit it again for many years.

Eventually, through the healing power of time and reflection, I "forgave" my grandparents for whatever transgression I had held them responsible for committing. Truly, there is no real way to know what causes schizophrenia, so there is no point in placing blame. The most important thing is just learning to deal with your current reality. Doing so will help you figure out how best to go on with your life.

CHAPTER 34

Vapors of the Past

Even as I built my own separate life, there were always reminders. Even now there were dreams of our childhood that returned to me unexpectedly, like vapors of the past—as if she was coming back to say hello.

After she was taken from me, I felt like a big slice was severed from my being, leaving a gaping, open wound. It left a hole in my heart so deep, I thought it could never be filled.

But I was wrong. Over time, the wound healed leaving only a painful scar.

Now it hurts less
Not like the knife that cut through me

Whenever I heard your name
Now my life goes on without you
And I only feel a dull pain
MGW

In rescued dusty boxes from the garage, I found the letters and small notebooks she wrote in, the papers now smelling old and decaying. On the aging pages among gibberish and spiders were pearls of beauty. The writing was precise and neat at first, her poetry shining through with bits of sophistication, her thoughts clearly articulated. She wrote poems that were eloquent and as clear as crystal, reflecting beauty inside and out.

Sunlight
It's one of those mornings
that comes bright and clear and warm.
Warmth that the sun is shining all the time.
And now we sit here
maybe learning something
and maybe I saw the sunlight in your eyes

Then over time, the writing loosened up and became incoherent, reflecting her loss of control and mental clarity.

Kathy was confused in her writing and thinking. She had an urgent need to analyze her innermost thoughts and place in the world. She had a driving compulsion to solve the societal problems she perceived around her. Yet, she was unable to first reconcile herself to her own inner conflicts and become comfortable with her own self. This caused a schism and breakdown that ultimately made it impossible for her to function in the world. She transferred her turmoil onto the people and situations of her life.

Many long years passed. So many that it sometimes felt like eons. Yet the past was always just within reach. It was captured in photos, in my mind's eye, and in those old dusty journals that were left lying neglected in the garage. Her journals and mine. Both of us wrote of loneliness and pain. She wrote poetry and prose, in notebooks, on her math assignments, crammed in wherever she could. Words from forty years back now rose up before me like a phoenix on the page.

At times, our writings seemed almost indistinguishable from each other and I wondered who was who.

May 1972

I am confused
Sometimes it's all right to feel
Sometimes it's very weird
When I had learned that I could only be feeling sometimes, I accepted. I could come in and out of my shell with ease. It was appreciated, and needed, I need to be needed and to feel loved, and to be held,
and so does everybody else and so I was very direct.

"Couldn't we just live together and facilitate each other's needs, gain love, and awareness of ourselves, share as we grow, without having to fear rejection and ridicule?"
I was very sure we could,
all we needed was each other.
But fear was there and I was exposed,
and now I may never come out again.
So I'm no longer sharing and I'm crying hard inside
when I see warmth attune to everything else,
not weird at all.
Somebody help me out please.
KG

And then there was my own wandering prose, laid bare on old, yellowing notebooks filled with doodled shapes in the margins and endless lament, as I struggled to find myself and to find love, just as she had.

I'm afraid. Afraid that I may never make it.
Never be great, never be anything.
Fine then. I will be nothing.
Me and You, Emily Dickinson.
Are you a nobody too?
Good, then there're two of us.
MG (and Emily Dickinson)

Your song is nicer with a smile
Your laughter brings me close

bring me close to you
Fear escapes me
worry melts
Your laughter brings me close to you
You're deeper than a well

This plastic cubicle smothers me
and I really need your eyes to shine
and let me know it's all right
I've heard so much senseless crying
this time I want out of the mold

I want to go into you
I want to fuse
and only I know and you know the way
to cut these ropes that keep me from relating to you

Our time is right
the pains undue
Let's break down walls
and start anew
MG

Self to Self-Fusion
When souls mingle
The shells of the ordinary are unimportant
We play in real emotion
keeping tune with one another

We leave the impenetrable icy blue and grey
eyes in their sockets

The source is easily found
and for as long as possible
we are removed from our lonely homes

We create a collective body
one with all
MG

ꕥ

That pain and longing never really goes away. It just sinks deeper into the bowels of your being and only rises up now and then. The memories rise up too, sometimes pleasantly and sometimes unbearably. Everything is still there. All the experiences of my life, the good and the bad, lie resting just below the surface, waiting for release.

After all the years that have passed, I still try to unravel the mystery of Kathy's illness. In one writing, a split personality is introduced.

Yes I believe I have two personalities. One is Francis, she has something to say...

Then the handwriting becomes different, scrawled, and shaky, like changing from right hand to left hand, as if it was written by someone else. The faded green ink looks ghostlike, rising up in a faint focus on the yellowed page, as if surfacing somewhere from deep within her subconscious.

Francis Wichaw...Need Glasses. Come over to see me—we are dreamer [arrow] *the weather is fabulous. She nice...*

PART THREE

Putting the Pieces Back Together

CHAPTER 35

Life Goes On

Take back the joy, feel it every day. Let your life go on in its own natural way. ~ MGW

ᔕᔓᔕ

"I will be happy to see you, dear."

The sound of my other grandmother's voice, still miles away, seemed close and familiar to me, like coming home. I kept driving up the coast, eager to begin my new life, the highway laid out before me like a sparkling ribbon. I was moving away from my childhood home and my past, on a mission to complete my college degree in a totally different locale.

Moving to Santa Cruz had come to me like an epiphany one day. I had completed only a year or two of college and was working in an aerospace factory on the swing shift. There was a whole other world inside that plant that I entered each day at 3:30 in the afternoon. The work was hard. The factory was filled with grit and noise. But I discovered camaraderie there among the workers that carried me through each day.

"*Marta, mi espousa hizo esto para tí, aquí estás.*"

Roberto handed me a huge homemade burrito wrapped in tin foil for my "lunch." It was still steaming hot and deliciously filling.

"*Muchas gracias a ustedes, Roberto. Qué delicioso!*"

During breaks, that were a mere ten minutes long, I sat at a picnic table, facing ladies as old as my own mother under the huge steel skeletons of airplanes towering above us. The riveting of metal echoed all around us. As these behemoths were wrapped in their metal skins, we gossiped and laughed, their hands stretching across the table toward me in an open gesture, sharing more than just friendly banter. It was a sisterhood of the working class.

As much as I enjoyed the company, I had grown tired of the routine and noise. I never intended to work there for long. Pausing one day as I lifted a box of parts onto the conveyor, it was suddenly clear to me. I could apply to UC Santa Cruz and reconnect with my father's mother, now a nun, who had lived there in the mountains for many years at a Catholic retreat house. I also had a few friends who lived there. Soon the epiphany turned into reality. I applied to UC Santa Cruz and was accepted. I made housing arrangements. I packed up my little car and headed north.

I finally arrived in Santa Cruz where I crashed in the living room of a friend until school started. A little house, shared with three women, just as I had done in high school, eventually became my home as I settled in at the university.

On the weekends, I drove up the curvy mountain road to visit my grandmother at St. Clara's retreat house. We would sit and visit in the cool basement apartment that she referred to as her "catacombs." On the wall was a corkboard covered with photos of her children, grandchildren, and great-grandchildren brought by family members who sometimes passed through.

"I'm getting used to that arm of yours."

Grandma Sister was leaning on me as I steadied her one side, the other buoyed by a cane. We walked across the expansive redwood deck of the retreat house as the sunlight filtered down from the surrounding forests. We ate lunch in a small private dining room and, afterward, I sat down at the small upright piano and muddled my way through a new Bartók piece I was learning as she nodded in appreciation.

"F sharp dear, not a natural."

She was a musician too, a pianist and organist. She

had reveled in the musical circles of her second husband, a conductor who she left my grandfather for. Yet she never gave up wanting to get her four little children back from him in a bitter and long battle. But it was my grandfather who gained custody, moving the kids around the state of Texas, so that she would not be able to find them.

After her second husband's death and her conversion to Catholicism, she worked as a housekeeper for some priests and then was accepted into a Franciscan order, starting her life over for a third time.

Those years were very special as I came to know her as friend. We could talk about just about everything and, one day, I even brought her to one of my women's studies classes, when the topic was grandmothers and granddaughters.

She looked stately in her black habit and I was proud to have her on my arm as we walked to class beneath the towering redwoods. The bond that grew between us was strong. She had reinvented herself and so had I. There was much to share.

And so life carried me along. I continued on my own path, staying in Santa Cruz after I graduated from college where I worked in a myriad of jobs and bought myself a small condo.

CHAPTER 36

Reconnecting

You can't make or will them to get well. Sometimes family is just too close to help. ~ MGW

ઌઌ

One Thanksgiving, I invited my family to come up, and I even cooked one of the turkeys that my employer had handed out for the holidays.

I still couldn't stop thinking about my sister and wondering if she would be better off moving to my area. I knew I didn't want her to live with me, even though she had often suggested it.

I knew I had to have my own life. But somehow, I

thought that, maybe in a smaller community with good mental health services, maybe, just maybe, things could be different for her.

After all that time in the maze of Los Angeles County, could such a move help her?

In a way, I was trying to do it for myself too, to stop the worrying, the agonizing, and some deep guilt that I couldn't seem to get past. I could not give up on my belief that I could somehow make things right again, if I only tried hard enough. I believed she would emerge from her illness as if stepping out of a tunnel, metamorphosed from the cocoon of all those years of pain and misery.

So I did my due diligence, researching the programs and board and care homes in the area, ending up with pages and pages of notes.

Kathy got a pass from her board and care facility and drove up with the family.

She had had her teeth removed on the dentist's recommendation and Dad had purchased expensive dentures, custom made for her but sadly she soon stopped wearing them. And so suddenly it seemed, there she was that Thanksgiving weekend, standing toothless on my front porch, tired from the long drive but happy to see me.

Home visits had always been challenging in the past. Kathy would drink coffee all night when she visited, giggle, and wander the halls. She had a smoker's cough that would keep everyone awake as she paced the house, giggling and coughing throughout the night.

But this would be the first time for her to visit me in my new home and I was determined to try and make it work. I had made some time for Kathy and me to drive around town, looking at some potential living environments.

We pulled up to a big, residential home near the ocean.

"Kathy, here's a place I thought you might be interested in living in."

"Well, maybe it's a place that *you* might be interested in."

Suddenly, Kathy became angry, resenting any suggestion I tried to make. She exited my car, slamming the door behind her then charged ahead of me toward the large stucco house.

Inside, a group of young people was lounging around the living room. A staffer showed us around the kitchen and the house.

"Hey, how you doing? You gonna move in here?"

The residents were mostly friendly and interested. One of the women stumbled past us and lay down limply on her bed.

"She don't want to talk."

We left that place and drove past another brightly painted apartment complex with some men hanging out in front, smoking.

"You could even have your own apartment here, Kathy."

"*You* could have your own apartment here!"

Things weren't going as well as I had hoped.

Our last stop was at a vocational center where a friend of mine worked. Clients came for the day and completed work projects—like mailings for local companies—worked in the garden, and were productive with their time while also participating in therapy and support groups.

Since it was Thanksgiving weekend, no one was there, except a social worker in a vividly bright tie-dyed dress with long flowing hair. Marilyn was skilled at drawing Kathy out as she told her about everything that went on there. She even encouraged Kathy to wear her false teeth, something I couldn't seem to do.

A few months later, my parents came to the area for a political and spiritual retreat and I arranged for them to drop Kathy off at my place on their way to the retreat. This time it would be just the two of us for the weekend.

We went to the hot tub garden where I worked as a volunteer. Kathy seemed at home with the nudity and we relaxed in the warm, soothing water, sipping lemon grass tea as the dusk settled into evening.

After dinner, I suggested we watch a movie. TV and movies hadn't interested her before and I never understood why, because I considered it a good way just to relax or an easy way for us to hang out together. Now I realize that it was because of the voices she heard. More competing voices must have made it worse, like torture inside her head.

But on this winter night we watched *Babette's Feast*, a French film with English subtitles. She loved it, and it was one of the few times she was able to focus. Maybe it was because we couldn't understand the French voices, that they were not distractions, pulling her down.

I could count that weekend as one of our happy times. Yet, in the end, Kathy said she wasn't ready for a move. My parents came for her and they all drove back to LA. It was where she felt at home, after all.

I was left to wonder if a move would really have made any difference in her life. I knew it would have changed mine forever. I would be the one getting the calls at 2 a.m. if she had a crisis or disappeared. Maybe I could have helped her, maybe not. Maybe I would have grown to hate her. This I would never know.

CHAPTER 37

A Child is Born

Kathy became pregnant during a stay in a state hospital. As her pregnancy progressed, she was transferred to San Pedro Peninsula Hospital in a beautiful location with a good psychiatric ward where she could also receive prenatal care.

Years later, I found a document stating the case for her involuntary commitment—a certification declaring that she was a danger to others due to "setting fires, urinating in her clothes, and not eating properly."

Although it was a forced hospitalization, it was one of the better facilities she had been admitted to, with an ocean view and a neighboring park with a large pond.

I went to visit as often as I could, flying or driving from Northern California.

We were allowed to leave the hospital and, together, we would sit in the sun next to the pond, not really knowing what to say, as Kathy tried to come to terms with her pregnancy.

The silence was filled with what we could not express in words—our longing to return to the past we had known, to return to the way things were, to be sisters once again. In the quiet, there was comfort, like a sad solace in our presence together.

After our day at the pond, I returned the following day to San Pedro and Kathy and I played Pac man on the free arcade in the psych ward, as we waited to start a counseling session with her concerned hospital social worker.

Mom, Kathy, the kind-faced counselor, and I were all sitting in a small, comfortable room, trying to get Kathy to open up.

"There's something I need to tell you all. I've been bleeding quite a bit."

The kind-faced counselor said that this could be normal but assured her that she would be examined that day.

After the baby was born and they were about to discharge her, the staff gave Kathy a little autograph book with a drawing of a baby lion cub on the front.

On the first page was a little poem written by a staff member:

June 19, 1983

As you wind your way through life
Though you encounter pain and strife
Remember that when you were here
There were those who held you dear
Good luck, Lance

The rest of the staff also wrote encouraging notes, wishing her well.

ꕥ

Marion was born on an Easter Sunday.
You wanted to call her "Mariah" like the wind
but that name was taken, swept away,
along with your child, wisped from your arms.

I was sitting on my mattress on the floor, talking on the phone as Kathy told me the joyful news of the birth after a long, hard pregnancy with an unknown outcome.

"I'm happy," she said, her voice beaming like any new mom.

My voice broke and tears rolled down my face. "I'm happy, too."

After a long and contentious court battle, Kathy lost custody of her child and a welcoming and loving family adopted the baby.

The psychiatric drugs in the infant's system led to

colic, a resulting hernia, and surgery, but she was lovingly cared for and she recovered.

Kathy didn't know it, but my mother and I saw that precious child occasionally until she was four and their family broke off contact with us.

That was not to be Kathy's only experience with motherhood. She became pregnant again, this time having a miscarriage.

Afterward, my parents brought her home for a rare overnight visit.

Being home made her settle back into a more comfortable past and she would beg to be able to move back there again, an obsession that slowed down any possible forward motion.

On this sad night, as dusk turned to dark within the familiar walls of the family home, Helen sat quietly beside Kathy as they both grieved for the child who they would never know.

Helen lovingly lit a candle for her grandchild and then passed the flame to Kathy who ignited her own candle. Tears were shed and prayers were said.

Kathy felt the comfort of her own mother's love. The relationship between them, once so volatile, had come full circle from a state of combat to one of comfort, from a mother to her hurting child, healing the enduring wounds that had kept them apart.

Kathy and Helen, 1996

CHAPTER 38

Calling Collect

You can focus and thrive in your own life and still love your sibling. ~ MGW

ఌఌ

As my own family circle joyfully grew, the likelihood of having Kathy move closer seemed more and more remote. I had married and was in the early throes of motherhood. As I lay with my baby at my breast and my husband beside me, I felt complete, like all the random jigsaw pieces of my existence finally fit together. I had a full and busy life full of challenges and I was relishing every moment of it.

I was immersed in my life, working full-time, managing my home and raising a toddler when the calls came.

Kathy could use and abuse the phone by calling collect and by tricking the operator into placing her calls, due to whatever emergency materialized from the vapors of her mind.

When I came home from work and found there were five to ten messages on the phone, I felt a sinking feeling in the pit of my stomach. I knew they had to be from her. I played them back and, as I listened to her going on and on about what I needed to do to take care of my daughter or to the hang-ups one after the other, I felt an impending sense of dread.

One day, she tracked down the sheriff's office near my house and told them my daughter was dead. They sent someone to my house to investigate and, when we were not home, spoke to my next-door neighbor. As in the past, I could not bring myself to explain to the kind lady next door that it was all just my sister's imagination gone wild.

When I found out what had happened, I felt horrified and violated. To have someone speak those words, to say my child was dead, even if it was only part of a paranoid fantasy, felt like someone was murdering *me* and threatening my family.

It was amazing that she could wreck such havoc from nearly 350 miles away just by picking up a receiver!

"I am very angry with you!" I told her my feelings emphatically, during our weekly call.

And then she said something she had never said to me before. "I'm sorry I am the way I am, Martha."

I was touched by her taking some responsibility, *finally*, for her actions. But in spite of her apology I knew I could no longer take the risk. The disruptive phone calls were harmful *to me* mentally and I knew I couldn't take them anymore.

The next time Kathy called the sheriff's office she told them my toddler had been left home alone. Maybe they were onto her because they called me instead of coming by.

"We are concerned for your welfare," said the conscientious woman on the phone as she investigated the incident. I finally got her to understand that it was all a false alarm.

Finally after a series of bizarre exchanges with the operator, Kathy got banned by my long distance service provider. Then she must have lost my phone number and I made sure not to give it to her again. After that, instead of calling me, Kathy called my parents on a daily basis, going into long diatribes that would frequently be recorded by their answering machine. This became like a sad and lonely therapy for her.

I still tried to make my weekly calls to wherever she was living.

"Martha, you need to buy Libbey's canned peas for Sabrina and Pampers diapers."

"But, Kathy, Sabrina is six years old now!"

I couldn't seem to get through to her, so I would just listen and then ask her about her day in the board and care. When the silence became too long and heavy, I finally brought the calls to a close by wishing her well.

CHAPTER 39

Bits of Happiness

Like many paranoid schizophrenics, Kathy seemed mostly concerned with herself, but there were times when her caring nature seemed to come forth. For Christmas, Dad gave her some money for presents and she went shopping at the thrift stores and outlets near her board and care in Los Angeles, carefully searching for special gifts for all her family members.

She bought my family a beautiful porcelain sugar and cream set painted intricately with blue and gold roses. The ornate handles have broken off over the years but the little sugar bowl still sits on our kitchen counter and does its job of sweetening my husband's coffee each morning.

She owned a big purple bathrobe that must have been

given to her and, one day, she offered to trade it to me for a less luxurious robe of mine. I know she was pleased when I accepted this "gift" and I cherish it to this day as a symbol of her love.

There were times when she seemed to be getting her life back. Like when she went to Las Vegas with the girls in her board and care home. And the summer she camped out in Santa Monica Canyon with a supportive group of peers from her counseling program. Everything seemed hopeful then, but when the program was cancelled, and she was moved elsewhere, she slipped back into the old psychiatric lethargy that held her down.

From the inner city board and care home where she ended up, she would walk across town and check herself in the psychiatric ward of a local hospital. It was here that a supportive doctor offered to get her into a special half-way house as a transition to everyday life, but Kathy refused the offer.

ᏋᏋ

"This is a nice place, better than the others," Dad told me as we drove to the latest residential hospital where Kathy had been placed.

Sure enough, it was. Although it looked like any other facility on the outside, inside there was a pool in the center of the facility and a beautiful Koi pond.

"Did you see the turtles?"

After we signed in, Kathy walked with me to the little pond and sat down to smoke in the atrium. We watched the turtles basking in the sun on their little rock islands and I almost forgot where we were. The residents of this place gained privileges to use the amenities through a point system. Yet, sadly, Kathy never advanced beyond the locked ward she was relegated to.

PART FOUR

Endings

CHAPTER 40

A Season for Loss

To everything, there is a season and a time to every purpose under heaven. ~ The Bible, Book of Ecclesiastes

ଓଠଓଠ

Mom and I had long since healed our relationship and kept in touch through visits and phone calls, when one day she phoned and I had a strange feeling. She said she was thinking of me and my husband Dan and the kind of people we were. Finally, she told me she wanted me to have a beautiful antique china cabinet that had been in our family for several generations. "I love you," she said as we finished the call.

"I love you too, Mom."

I paused after hanging up the phone, thinking of her as I went about my day. *Something must be up*, I thought.

A week later, I received another phone call.

"Helen had a stroke." As usual Dad's words were concise and to the point.

He sounded hopeful and I tried to expect the best. After all, people had strokes every day.

That night, I dreamed about her. I was at an opulent fancy place, like a hotel, and Kathy and I were waiting for Mom to make an appearance. We saw a beautiful, white silk dress in a store window, then Mom emerged wearing it and looking gorgeous. A group of people were gathered on a dock nearby, all to honor her and perhaps to see her off. She made an entrance then walked down the dock, waving to the assembled crowd, and then departed on a boat.

It was a beautiful dream but it left me fearful about the outcome of this illness. Would Mom be leaving us, after all?

By the next evening, she was unresponsive and bordering on comatose and so I quickly booked a flight. I was relieved to see her but full of anxiety because she was not conscious most of the time. Everyone was saying how *well* she was doing. What on earth were they talking about? Couldn't they see that she was *dying*? I paced the hall and sat on the couch, but then I wanted to be at her side again. *I need my mom!* As the tears welled up, I could hear my inner child crying plaintively, *I want my mommy!*

As her condition worsened, they transported her from the nursing facility to the hospital, wheeling her to a waiting ambulance. The dismal, gray rain darkened the day like an eclipse, filled with despair. Our family reassembled at the hospital and, in a private conversation off the emergency ward, one doctor leveled with me, telling me she might never recover to a higher level than the one she was at now.

I looked at Mom and she was suddenly fully conscious. She cocked her head toward the hospital machinery and shrugged, with an air of nonchalance. There was a look of acceptance on her face. Her eyes twinkled. Even though she might not be able to speak again, I knew she was *still there* and the same person inside that she had always been.

The doctor who leveled with me turned out to be right. My witty mother, the writer, teacher, and community activist, the pillar of our family, would never regain her full verbal ability or use of her left side. She was taken back to the comfortable nursing home with the sunny patio to a room that she shared with two other pleasant ladies who would later pass away.

ຯຯ

Dad and I walked past some towering tropical palms

and entered the Monarch Nursing Facility where my mother had lived for three years now. It was a very good place, the best that his money could buy. Yet nothing could mask the forlornness of those with little hope, or the faint smell of urine, mixed with chicken soup, that permeated the halls as we walked past still-life paintings of landscapes, and flowers in bright colors, that endeavored to cheer the walls.

Mom mostly kept a bright demeanor although she sometimes got discouraged and cried in frustration. I watched one afternoon as she wheeled herself up and down the hallways by clutching on to the side rails with her good arm. She was wearing a pink pinstriped housecoat as her matching pink-slippered feet slid along the linoleum floor.

Thanks to the resident beauty salon, her snowy soft curls were neatly coiffed and her nails were done with clear shiny nail polish. She reached out and grasped the hands of the patients she passed with a soft, healing touch that seemed to be appreciated by the others, some of whom were lonely and forgotten.

One ashen-faced and crumpled man raised his head in surprise. I saw a light return to his eyes as she took his hand and he gazed back at her, seeming astonished to find that someone cared.

Visitors were frequent from a supportive group of friends that tried to help her regain her abilities. We read to her and showed her photos of the family, repeating our names, writing words on a white board as we showed her corresponding pictures, waiting for her to repeat the words or say something, anything.

But most of the time only gibberish comes out.

"Spankety-spank," Helen said. "Makin' bacon."

As time went on, we were all just happy to be there with her.

Life continued to go forward in this way. My father was devoted and loyal, even going so far as to buy a special car to transport her home for holiday visits and trips to the nearby park and nature center.

Dad faithfully drove to see her two, or even three times a day. When I visited, I sometimes brought my four-year-old daughter—who one day dressed up like a princess, wearing a crown, strolling regally into Mom's room, which was so full of photos, cards, hanging origami, and other knick-knacks that there was hardly any space left to sit down.

Mom's face brightened at the sight of her granddaughter. Then she suddenly turned and placed her hand softly on the side of my face, uttering one of the most complete sentences spoken since her stroke, as clear as day. "Martha is my daughter."

Sitting in the sunny patio with her the next day, I reflected on everything we had gone through and on how much I loved this woman. I remembered my teenage rebelliousness and defiance, of the times we said hurtful things—the seesaw relationship of parent and child, mother and daughter.

I knelt down next to her wheelchair, took her hand, and looked deep into her pale blue eyes.

"I'm sorry for all the things I did, Mom, for what I put you through."

Suddenly, all the anger and pain of the past seemed to melt away like sun chasing away the fog. As she gently cradled my face with her good hand and held my gaze with her light blue sparkling eyes, I knew we both were forgiven.

ᏣᏣ

As the years passed, when I told my friends and coworkers about my mother, everyone seemed to feel so sorry and incredulous, as if it was hard to believe my family could continue to go on coping after all this time. They didn't understand about the love between us. How could I explain that my parents were actually happy together, that they were continuing to share this chapter in their lives as they had all the other equally enduring episodes of the past fifty years?

But like every love story, the ending came. Five years after her stroke, following several medical crises, I found myself again in that small room. I was joined by my brothers on the side of her hospital bed, waiting for her life to come to a close, jotting down thoughts on my palm pilot from time to time.

In the lobby, scenes played out on television of the death and destruction brought by Hurricane Katrina as my mother lay dying. I watched as desperate people clung to rooftops struggling not to drown. I felt I was drowning too as death churned around us, lapping at us like the flood waters from that great storm. I felt tremendous empathy for their suffering while I witnessed my mother suffering on a different level, as her body slowly began to shut down and her face winced in pain.

We waited at death's door,
But death was not kind.
She took her time.

Morphine finally helped to make her more comfortable and now she looked humble and peaceful, as the long hours passed and visitors came and went. Then our family encircled her, holding hands as she released her last breath with grace and dignity. We were brought closer by the intimacy of death. At home, we sat up late into the night talking, crying, and reminiscing. For she was gone.

CHAPTER 41

Well of Grief

As Dad and I entered the psychiatric facility to see Kathy, I was filled with trepidation. I knew we would be telling Kathy about Mom's death, but also this place felt hopeless to me. It was one of the worst ones—patients were milling about long halls with open doors. It was noisy and disorganized. We met with Kathy in a drab lounge. I noticed a cartoon-like drawing on the bulletin board and recognized it as one of her drawings of a small, carefree figure, and I praised her for it.

Kathy was withdrawn. Her dark hair was dirty and uncombed, her clothes unkempt. This was neither a good place nor a happy time. We had brought her a chicken sandwich.

Before too long, Dad gave her the news. “Helen died yesterday.”

Kathy was quiet and stopped eating the sandwich. “This is like the sandwiches Mom made.” Her words hung in the air. Then she broke down. “Why did she have to die?”

I wrapped my arms around my sister in comfort. “I know! We loved her so much.”

Both of us cried a bit, drawing from a shared well of grief in that small, gray room.

When it was time to leave, I told the nurse that Kathy’s mom had just died, hoping they would show some extra kindness to her. I was sorry and sad to leave her there, but it wouldn’t be long before she returned to the Button Street board and care, where she had lived before and considered a real home. A place where she felt safe and well cared for.

CHAPTER 42

Final Acts

If you have a sister and she dies, do you stop saying you have one? Or are you always a sister, even when the other half of the equation is gone?

~ Jodi Picoult, *My Sister's Keeper*

∽∽

One Christmas, Kathy did not shop for gifts for our family, even though Dad provided her with an allowance for this purpose. The whole family drove to Los Angeles to visit her—Dad, Charlie, John, and I. Mom was the missing link. We went out to eat at Kathy's favorite restaurant.

Looking around the table at each of us, she told us

what she planned to give us. "Old Spice Cologne," she announced to my brothers, as if she were presenting a carefully wrapped package.

They graciously accepted their virtual gifts. "Thank you."

A sweater for me, a toy for my daughter, something for Dad—all of it was carefully planned. It was touching, since we all sensed that this was to be her last loving act for us.

That year, she became afraid that Dad would pass away and leave her alone. When I visited, the three of us sat in that same restaurant. She pressed a card into my hand with her social worker's name, and Kathy's social security number scrawled across the back. I told her she could move to Northern California to live near me but sensed this would not happen. Dad tried to reassure her that she would not be abandoned, but her sadness and uneasiness were clear.

It was during that year, during one of our weekly phone calls, that she began to talk about dying.

"I've decided it would be better if I died."

"Lots of people love you, Kathy."

I tried to soothe her, but things went rapidly downhill from there.

During a hospitalization, I tried to talk to her on the phone but on the other end there was only guttural muttering. I said goodbye and hung up, mortified at her mental deterioration.

ᘓᘐᘓᘐ

I strode purposefully through the gift shop in the mall in Maui, at the tail end of our family vacation. I *had* to find her something. I *needed* to find Kathy a gift for her birthday that was a week away. Something she might like and even appreciate. Finally, I settled on a T-Shirt with a tropical print on the front.

As soon as we returned home, I immediately headed to the post office and mailed the present, along with a birthday card, into which I stuffed a ten-dollar bill. I felt compelled by something urgent inside, knowing it was vital that she receive it by her birthday.

On her birthday, on August twenty-second, I called Button Street where she was living again, back in familiar surroundings. But Kathy had turned away from her family, refusing to see even my Dad, her most loyal visitor. She had turned a corner and cut herself off, heading on alone.

"Happy birthday, Kathy." I tried to infuse my voice with love and joy, relived that I had reached her in time.

"You're not supposed to call me! Never call me again!"

The click on the other end struck me like a final blow. I carried on with my day—sad, but feeling like I had done all I could. Dad tried to visit her that day, but she turned him away, although I was relieved when he told me that she had received my package.

CHAPTER 43

Heat Kills—The Hardest Chapter

The heat was stiffening and lethal at the end of the summer of 1997. It hung over the Los Angeles basin and its outlaying communities in a suffocating blanket of triple-digit temperatures for nearly a week.

As the Labor Day weekend approached, more and more people succumbed to the deadly heat wave, their stories filling the local papers and television news. An elderly couple, a twenty-six-year-old man whose dirt bike broke down, a woman living out of her car, the elderly, the homeless, undocumented immigrants, shut-ins, the mentally ill, people without protection from the elements, those living on the edge. Many would die alone and neglected—all victims of a silent killer.

My own sister Kathy's life was also to be lost in the end, not by the schizophrenia that had plagued her for so many years, but by another invisible foe—climate change and its extreme weather events—leaving us, her family, as survivors of two tragedies. I reflected back to the sad time of Mom's death during Hurricane Katrina, two years before, and of all those survivors who we now stood with—the growing numbers worldwide who had and would sadly perish from this man-made specter.

Although I found very little comfort in these thoughts, later they would motivate me to fight for change.

That morning, Labor Day, September 3, 2007, Dad had called, awakening us. "Kathy died last night."

I broke down. Not knowing where to take the grief that shook the core of my being, I stumbled to the bathroom, still clutching the phone. I pulled on the purple robe that she had given me and stumbled through the house, sobbing hysterically as the flood gates of over thirty years of heartache were let loose.

I staggered to front door, through a thickness surrounding me, and sat on the front porch swing in the cool air of that gray morning, crying and crying, still talking to Dad. I was glad he stayed there for me and that Dan came and put his arms around me.

When I came back into the house, my daughter had woken up and wanted to know what was wrong. I sat down next to her, the sobs still wracking my body, and told her that my sister, her only aunt, was dead.

I lost my fifty-one-year-old sister on that fateful Labor Day holiday. She died in the little Button Street home, her decades-long struggle with mental illness brought to a tragic close. And although both heart disease and the heat were later counted as her statistical killers, on that day, she joined the growing number of victims of extreme weather, a sad testament of our times.

The end came in one of her hardest times, after she had given into the psychosis that always lingered around her, letting it overtake her, giving into its dark whims. She had cut herself off from the family, refusing to see us. She was wearing multiple layers of clothing as a psychological defense and protection from the world. Although her caregivers had urged her to remove the clothing, she refused and the resulting hyperthermia played a major role in her death.

I immediately flew home. When Dad picked me up at the airport, he showed me the newspaper articles that told the stories of the deaths that had taken place that week. We stopped to make some copies for our relatives. Maybe it would make it easier to explain what had happened.

When we got to the house, I did online searches, which led me to a television newscast about Kathy that had just aired. The woman reporter stood outside the Button Street home, implicating the owners for not having air conditioning. Then Kathy's picture was superimposed on the screen, her face looking puzzled and aloof on some photo ID that must have been obtained from the DMV. Still in shock, I could hardly believe what I was seeing.

A worker at the home recounted to the camera how they used fans to cool the place and described in detail how Kathy had insisted on wearing too much clothing, refusing to remove them by saying, "It's my right."

I thought back to our last conversation when she yelled at me, furious for calling her, and I realized that the little Button Street home should not be blamed. She had been like someone on a hunger strike, and it was clear to me that Kathy had made her own decision. It would have been nearly impossible to reason with her in such a psychotic state.

All I could feel was sadness, grief, and a sense of finality. I had always known this day might come but, now that it had, I struggled to accept that she was gone.

ɕɔɕɔ

"Kathy was cremated."

Dad informed me curtly of this fact shortly after she passed away. With a sinking feeling, I contemplated the finality of his statement. What had been done could never be changed. There had been an autopsy but not of her brain. Now we would never know more about her condition and its organic origins. I thought of the pleas from the National Alliance on Mental Illness for donations of brains from the deceased. Why had we never discussed this? Plans were made for a memorial on the long Thanksgiving weekend when relatives would be able to attend.

CHAPTER 44

In Memoriam

If your sibling dies, be sure to seek grief counseling through hospice or another organization. You can focus and thrive in your own life and still honor and love your sibling. What happened to them is not your fault. You have your own fate and life course to follow. ~ MGW

ᘓᘐ

It was a beautiful November morning, under sunny Southern California skies, when my brother Charlie and I arrived at the church grounds to set up for Kathy's memorial. As we stepped out onto the open grassy area, where we used to play as children, there suddenly appeared a large hawk high above us. A solitary speck in the sky, it slowly came into clearer view, circling above the green lawn surrounding the old pepperwood tree, framed by the large beamed sculpture, which dominated the grounds. We stood and silently watched its graceful spirals, reveling in the quiet perfection of the moment, our thoughts turning to our sister and our tasks for the day.

In the spacious sunlit lounge, we opened the patio doors wide. Within moments, a large yellow butterfly flew in and fluttered around the room. I thought of all the workshops, lessons, and parties that had transpired in that very room and saw in my mind a vivid memory of Kathy twirling around the floor in a joyous dance as she turned toward me, as if to give me that joy as a comforting gift.

❧❧

It was 1972 and our parakeets were in their white cage on the front porch, reveling in the sun and fresh air, chirping to their hearts' content. Suddenly, the front door opened wide, striking the cage, which careened to the ground with the top and bottom falling apart. As Kathy and I stood by helplessly, there was a flash of color as two little spots of green and blue sped by in an instant, flying out to the yard and then soaring up high, past the evergreens that lined our street—tiny bright specks that finally disappeared into the blue sky.

Kathy ran into the street and stood gazing upward, watching our pets escape to freedom and an almost certain death. She seemed relived and resigned as she turned back to face me. "They are free now, Martha."

ᏋᏜᏋᏜ

My attention returned to the lounge and the reality of this day. But the butterfly and the hawk's flight, like the escaped parakeets of our childhood, all harkened back to Kathy and the release of her mind from earthly bounds, even back then. It was all so perfectly symbolic of Kathy and the freedom of her spirit.

As I thought of her, I felt a comforting release, a release of pain and suffering, a final flight of her spirit in joy. I held tightly to this sensation as the room slowly filled with our cousins and friends and we shared our recollections of the sister, cousin, daughter, and friend who we all loved so much.

She is a Memory
A whirl of energy,
a mischievous grin.
Living, laughing, loving,
and the world loved her in return.
Too soon her gift was taken,
before her mark on the world was complete
and then she struggled on and on in pain.

So now it's time to let her go.
She is a memory
of the happiness of a family
in a magical place enshrined
She is a Memory of Love.

As I read the poem I wrote for her memorial, many kind words and precious memories were shared. In the ensuing weeks that turned into months, I continued to process the multiple layers of my grief and work through bouts of depression by seeing a caring grief counselor offered graciously by hospice. I created a memorial website for Kathy that was appreciated by family and friends and that brought me some comfort.

Slowly, I started to feel an increasing sense of closure, as I looked back on our lives together, knowing I needed to move on with my own life.

ೞೞ

After she passed, we poured over the childhood photos—the happy faces and magical experiences of our youth. I appreciated the great efforts my parents took to expose us to nature and to enriching activities, as I now tried to do with my own daughter. The circle continued, unbroken.

Mom had lovingly created photo albums for each of us. When I looked through mine, the first part was full of

Kathy and me—little girls, sisters, doing all the things little girls do. Then, the album changed and Kathy slowly seemed to drop out of my life. I knew this was after she got sick, after the years in state mental hospitals and board and care homes. And I knew that at the same time I was dealing with this, I was also refocusing my life. More photos appear of my best friend, of the things we did together—like going to Hawaii every summer to stay with her family. She became like a sister to me. Photos of her and other friends, my accomplishments, and places I visited filled the remainder of the album.

I filled my life with other things, other people, so as not to dwell in the pain and so that I could survive emotionally, but also to fulfill my own life's purpose. But she was never far from me.

ꕥꕥ

A year and a half would pass before I finally got up the courage to write the LA coroner and request a copy of Kathy's autopsy. I set aside the large envelope after it came in the mail. Then on a Saturday afternoon when I was alone, I took a deep breath and finally opened it.

As I read it, I broke down. Kathy had heart disease, which was listed as the main cause of her death. Hyperthermia from the record-breaking heat wave was listed as a secondary cause of death. I felt confused and shocked. Also attached was the police report. This, saddest of all, was written almost eloquently by Officer McCabe, who seemed to truly care about his job of understanding her death. He described the scene at the board and care home where she died in detail. How her body lay in a "supine" position on the floor between two beds. How the paramedics cut away her excessive clothing, including heavy fleece vests and two heavy weight jackets. How "the room is warm and stuffy on this hot summer evening. There is no sign of foul play." She had been observed alive and sleeping on the floor an hour earlier on one of the hottest days in LA history.

It was all there, all the morbid details of death, down to drawings and numbers. How her liver temperature was 104 even two hours after her death. The high level of the psychiatric drug in her system was referred to as "clozapine intoxication."

Did she lie down hoping to die? I wondered, knowing that she had given up on living, that she had told us so over the past year, that she had decided it would be better to die than go on living without much hope of ever getting better.

As I finished reading this tragic, true story about my very own sister, I found myself thinking, *Does anyone really care about this death?* My own torrent of tears answered as I sobbed to myself, "I care, I care! God, I loved her!"

CHAPTER 45

Unexpected Comfort

The following is a Poem by Birago Diop (1906-1989), Senegalese author and veterinary surgeon.

The dead are not gone forever.
They are in the paling shadows,
And in the darkening shadows.
The dead are not beneath the ground,
They are in the rustling tree,
In the murmuring wood,
In the flowing water,
In the still water,
In the lonely place, in the crowd:
The dead are not dead.

Loss in life comes fast and hard. To some it comes early and harsh, while for most of us, the longer we live, the more loss we experience. I expected my mother's death but not my sister's, that came, while maybe not unanticipated, as shocking and brutal as striking a brick wall. Then suddenly, it seemed, they were both gone. A third of my family had passed away, leaving me as the lone female survivor.

As time went on and I muddled through my grief, I soon found comfort in the return of vivid memories etched deep within my soul.

I believe those who have passed leave messages for us, which are there when we need them the most, if we are open to receiving them. Or so it happened to me…

ɛɔɛɔ

It was the beginning of January, four months after Kathy's death. Coming out of a long, two-week family holiday, I felt tired and in a post-Christmas slump. I suggested that our family go out to breakfast. By the time we got there, I was feeling hungry and crabby. For most of the day, I couldn't shake this feeling of being tired, stressed, and annoyed, plus not liking myself for being this way. I stared off into space. I felt that my emotions were very obvious to the rest of the world, my heart as usual, resting prominently upon my sleeve.

After breakfast, we picked up some baskets to organize our bedroom. After my daughter and husband went out to take her friend home, I started the dreary task of going through my bedside cabinet to clear it of stuff. I was going through old letters, pictures, and mementos when I came across a picture of Kathy. She was smiling and holding a guitar, sitting on a boulder in my parent's front yard. I almost spoke out loud, saying "hey" or "hi" to her. The memory was fresh and clear and I was happy to see her image there in front of me.

Then I came across some letters she had written me. An inner voice warned, "Now it's time for the tears." But there would be no tears this time. She had written to me that she felt closer to me than ever, even though we were far apart.

And then she wrote, "Thank you for being Martha, Martha."

The simple, sweet message soothed me like a balm soothing an ache, drying the tears that still came when I thought of the sadness of her life.

Then, right there, in the same drawer, I pulled out some letters from my mom, Helen, the prolific, wordy writer of the family. They were also filled with appreciation and praise of me.

One of the letters had been sent from China, thanking me for the hologram stickers I gave to my parents, to give away when they were there. She also appreciated how I hosted them on a visit to my place and mentioned the different dishes I had prepared.

I realized I inherited her love of entertaining—the planning and cooking—especially after this holiday. I was becoming more and more like my mom and I was glad for this. I had unknowingly emulated the best things about her—her kindness and caring for others.

My mood had lightened, like light breaking through my mental fog. What were the odds that I would come across these words left behind by my sister and mother now when I was most in need of them? I was comforted by these pieces that fell into place helping me on my way.

CHAPTER 46

Anniversaries, Birthdays and Dreams

Grief Tides

Grief ebbs and flows like the tide.
It rushes across the shore, drawing me in.
Then pulls back some more,
Leaving empty shells and patterns in the sand.
I contemplate its absence,
Recall the tempest of its arrival,
And await its watery return.

I continued to write in my journal as I always had, sorting through my grief and dreams. I even wrote letters to my mother and sister as a form of healing self-therapy.

January 11, 2008:

I dreamed of Kathy last night. The two of us were sitting on a rock, in the sun out in nature with our backs together, like bookends, just being there. I felt very soothed when I woke up. It felt like another comforting message or visit from her, or a journey back to the past.

ભ૭ભ૭

March 31, 2008:

This morning during twilight sleep, I thought of Kathy. The tragedy grabbed at my heart yet again. I had an image of myself reaching up with one hand and grasping at her spirit as it left the earth, as if to say "Hey, come back! Let's try it all again. Let's give your life another go here on this earthly plane where you are loved."

I wish I could have helped her some more and taught her to feel good about herself. I know I tried, we tried. There could have been more for her. And I was left with this aching in my soul—a loss that many others had known.

ભ૭ભ૭

May 30, 2008 (My mother, Helen's, birthday was yesterday)

Dear Mom,

Yesterday was your birthday and we thought of you

with love. You still inspire me with your selfless acts of kindness and I strive to be like you. Lately I've been thinking about your life. I know it was a hard life even though you were not one to complain. Your past must have been painful and sad, having lost all your immediate family, two of them to alcoholism and mental illness but these are things we never discussed. I wish now that we had talked more about so many things.

Mom, it amazes me how much our lives are alike now. I am dependent on my husband's income now as you were. This was a hard fact for me to adjust to but for your generation it was the norm. We both are raising children although I only have one.

I can only imagine how hard it was raising four. I understand the frustration you faced as a writer as you strove to realize your dream of writing a book. But this ended up taking second place to us, your family. I'm glad you got to finally be just Helen with Jack, with no demanding kids around, except for Kathy with her emotional needs.

You can be proud of all the work you did. You were there for Kathy in her dark times and you gave all of us such a strong foundation. You were greatly loved and appreciated by the community that you gave so much to.

Mom, I'm glad for this time in my life to reflect and walk a path like yours. I know you are walking beside me. I love you always.

ෆෆ

August 22, 2008

I think of you in the morning.
My thoughts surfacing from the still waters of sleep.
Remembering, missing, yearning,
Wondering at my loss of you.
The sadness is like a cloak I struggle beneath.
Just wondering what you could have been,
If you had only stayed here with us

ෆෆ

Dear Kathy,

Today is your birthday. You would have been 52. I know you never liked aging. The added years were a reminder for you of all the things you could not have. But I would like to celebrate your birth, your life, and the sister who I loved on this day, not the anniversary of your death eleven days from now. Better to remember the child who was treasured, the girl who laughed, and the older sibling who taught me how to press on in the world, making my own impression. Please know how much you were and are loved. Forgive me for hurting you as I forgive the pain you brought to me. You will always be my sister. I miss you.

Love, Martha

CHAPTER 47

Sad Septembers

The following is a song by Phil Ochs.

Sit by my side, come as close as the air,
Share in a memory of gray;
And wander in my words, dream about the pictures
That I play, of changes.
Green leaves of summer turn red in the fall
To brown and to yellow they fade.
And then they have to die, trapped within
the circle time parade of changes.
Scenes of my young years were warm in my mind,
Visions of shadows that shine.
'Til one day I returned and found they were the
Victims of the vines of changes.

ఆఆ

August 29, 2008:

Kathy would sing this haunting Phil Ochs tune while she strummed her guitar, her voice echoing sadly, and now, it seemed, prophetically. But just like his songs, her poetry and the impressions of her life were left behind and brought me comfort.

Every autumn brought sadness, along with the brown leaves like Phil Ochs' song. Kathy's birthday was last week. Now the death anniversaries approach: Mom's on September first and Kathy's the next day. Helen's death fell next to the anniversary of Hurricane Katrina and then the final blow of the September eleventh remembrance would round out this period of fading leaves, my mosh pit of grief.

ఆఆ

September 1, 2008:

Today was the three-year anniversary of my Mother's death. Tomorrow was also the one-year marker of Kathy's death, which still felt raw to me, like a wound that was slowly closing up. I knew the pain, the tender scar would always remain but I owned it—my scar, my pain, my love for them that I would always carry.

I had reconciled myself to this strange coincidence—my sister dying two years and one day after my mother and, eventually, found the thought of the two of them, together in death, to be of comfort to me. But this strange anniversary, of a double death, now and forever more, had been more painful that I could have imagined. Tears had welled up with the thought of them and of others who were suffering. Talking with my own daughter, I had felt like crying for no reason other than that I loved her so much.

So how did I spend today? It felt good in the end. As the heat of the day faded into the golden glow of late afternoon, I tended to my plants, carefully watering and misting them. I harvested little fingerling potatoes from my garden. What a thrill to find the little babies beneath the soil! I felt good, connected to the earth and celebrating life. So after all the emotional anticipation, it was a celebration of life for my mom, remembering her as I went about my life, treasuring her harvest, too.

ɞɞ

August 21, 2009:

I dreamed of Kathy last night. Tomorrow would be her birthday. She would be fifty-three. And I was fifty-one, the same age as when she died. I didn't remember too much about my dream, just that she was dying or had decided to die. At the place we were, no one could really help, it was just accepted that this would happen. She died peacefully and I remembered seeing her lying still and tranquil. Then I went into a room to be by myself in my period of mourning.

Waking up, I did not feel the pain of grief, just acceptance as if this was how it must be. I wonder now, if someone wants to die, if they have a horrible illness as she did, should we let them go? My mind says yes but my heart says no.

ꕥ

September 2, 2009:

It had been two years today since Kathy died and the four year anniversary of Mom's death was yesterday. I had to say it was easier this year to cope. I didn't feel like I was hitting a brick wall of depression. Yesterday I felt sad but I tried to hold Mom in the light and asked her to guide me. I tried to help a friend whose mother died a month ago and this felt like the right thing to do.

As for Kathy, the dream I had recently seemed to set a tone of acceptance that I was able to bear more easily. I felt tremendous empathy for all families who struggled under similar circumstances and for those that were grieving in the midst of loss.

EPILOGUE

I believe those who have passed away leave much behind for us, the living. There are the memories and dreams so vivid you can almost touch them. There are the moments when I hear their voices rising up inside me as if they never left.

My mother speaks to me in the kitchen. “Mouse.”

I hear her speak my nickname in my mind, lovingly and softly.

That voice came out of nowhere to me one day. I smiled, remembering her and how much she loved me. I welcome this greeting from her that makes me realize that she is still with me, walking alongside me in my life, looking on.

My grandmother calls me “missy” and laughs her hearty laugh.

She was always so happy to see us and opened her

arms in welcome when we arrived at her three-story Texas home.

The letters and journals my sister left behind are full of messages to me now, catapulted to me in the present:

Martha, I'm so proud of you. You started from scratch and now you have a new car and a house—your own. And you did it all on your own (little mouse sister!) I'm so proud of you! You work hard for your living. I only want you to enjoy it and be happy.

I remember how Kathy was so happy for me for creating a family and how she wanted me to experience all the joy in my life that I could.

She lived vicariously through me and shared the joys and triumphs of my life from afar, and I like to think that she always will.

Kathy with guitar, Christmas 1984

Honor your sibling by living your own life to the fullest. Cherish the memories, mourn for the lost promise but embrace the now. ~ MGW

Author's Note

I did not want to write this book.

When I lost my sister soon after the death of my mother, the thought of writing about those painful years was so daunting that I avoided the very idea of it. I turned away, hoping to escape from my past and my own internal scrutiny. Maybe I could write a children's book or short stories? Something happy and carefree—anything to escape the deep emotional journey that called out to me.

But as time passed, the memories of my sister and the life we shared trickled down like drops from a spring, slowly wearing away my resistance like water wears away a rock. As the droplets continued cascading into a persistent flood, refusing to leave me alone, I realized that I could not ignore them or go on without examining them.

Stubborn questions tugged at me, refusing to let go. What was the meaning behind my sister's life and my life in connection to her? For I firmly believe we are all placed on this earth for a special, unique purpose. What did she leave behind and what was the meaning behind the gifts she left us? I realized that I wanted to share my journey with others who have felt the impact of mental illness in their families.

I began to write in spurts, extracting images from my soul, one painful twist at a time. I grasped at the chunks of memories, throwing them down upon paper and finally stitched them together into a tattered tapestry. Luckily, I found that once the memory spout was opened, lots of good memories surfaced too, making me grateful for the richness of my past. Once the memories were uncovered, I knew could revel in them forever. As I wrote it all down on paper, I felt unburdened and relieved as if I exhaled a breath that I had been holding in for decades.

As if to spur me on, I discovered a treasure trove of my sister's writing and poetry along with my own, stashed away in cardboard boxes in my parents' garage which I rescued and foraged through. I shared some of these early writings in this book as a testament to her brief but profound life, connecting our past to the present and even the future.

The long process of writing this book was nurtured by the amazing online community of writers and memoirists who inspired me daily. I am grateful for every encouraging word. I also want to thank all the good people at Black Opal Books for believing in me and my story. And special thanks to my family and friends for their unconditional love and support.

It is my wish that this book serve as a guide and touchstone for anyone experiencing similar turmoil in their lives. It is a voice for them—the voice that I wish I had had. It is a voice for all siblings and family members who have struggled with mental health issues, to encourage them to reclaim their own lives and inner joy. After all, surviving and thriving while going on with your own life is the best way to honor your sibling as well as yourself. I hope my story will resonate with others and help them to reclaim their own memories, both painful and joyous, along the way.

RESOURCE GUIDE

Mental Health Resources

National Suicide Prevention Lifeline
1 (800) 273-8255
www.suicidepreventionlifeline.org

National Alliance on Mental Illness, offers a free Family-to-Family 12 week course
Help Line 800-950-6264
www.nami.org

Project LETS is a non-profit organization, educational program, and movement dedicated to eliminating the stigma associated with mental illness and suicide in middle schools and high schools.
www.letserasethestigma.com

Sibling Support Project
http://www.siblingsupport.org/

http://www.schizophrenia.com

www.bringchange2mind.org

www.eachmindmatters.org

Siblings Network for Brothers and Sisters (England)
www.rethink.org

Climate Change Resources

www.NextGenClimate.org

www.ClimateParents.org

www.environmentalsciencedegree.com/climate-change

About the Author

Martha Graham-Waldon is a writer, spiritual entrepreneur and armchair activist who happily resides in the Santa Cruz Mountains of California with her family and a menagerie of pets. Her articles have been published locally, online and internationally. She is a winner of the Women's Memoirs 2015 contest for a vignette adapted from this memoir. A member of the National Association of Memoir Writers, Martha also loves travel, the outdoors, Jazzercise and music.